PEOPLE'S BIBLE COMMENTARY

OBADIAH/ JONAH/MICAH

CYRIL W. SPAUDE

PBC

CONCORDIA PUBLISHING HOUSE · SAINT LOUIS

CONTENTS

ILLUSTRATIONS

MAPS

Editor's Preface

The *People's Bible Commentary* is just what the name implies—a Bible and commentary for the people. It includes the complete text of the Holy Scriptures in the popular New International Version. The commentary following the Scripture sections contains personal applications as well as historical background and explanations of the text.

The authors of the *People's Bible Commentary* are men of scholarship and practical insight gained from years of experience in the teaching and preaching ministries. They have tried to avoid the technical jargon which limits so many commentary series to professional Bible scholars.

The most important feature of these books is that they are Christ-centered. Speaking of the Old Testament Scriptures, Jesus himself declared, "These are the Scriptures that testify about me" (John 5:39). Each volume of the *People's Bible Commentary* directs our attention to Jesus Christ. He is the center of the entire Bible. He is our only Savior.

We dedicate these volumes to the glory of God and to the good of his people.

The Publishers

INTRODUCTION TO OBADIAH

With only 21 verses, Obadiah is the shortest book in the Old Testament. But this brevity in no way diminishes the book's importance. Obadiah was the first prophet to use the term "the day of the LORD" (verse 15). Except for Moses, who is in a class by himself, Obadiah was also the first literary, or writing, prophet. Nathan, Samuel, and the other prophets who preceded him were not directed by the Lord to put their utterances in writing.

Although Obadiah is thought to have lived and written earlier than the prophet Amos, in both the traditional as well as in the Hebrew arrangement of the books of the Old Testament, Obadiah is placed after Amos. Some scholars believe this was done by the men who assembled the books of the Old Testament canon because they may have regarded Obadiah as an expansion of the short prediction against Edom in Amos 9:12. Obadiah is not quoted in the New Testament unless Revelation 11:15 is an indirect reference to verse 21 of Obadiah.

Author

The name Obadiah means "servant of Jehovah, or Jahweh" and is a somewhat common name in the Old Testament. Attempts have been made to identify the author of this book with one of the more than ten Obadiahs mentioned in the Old Testament. But we simply do not know who his parents were or where he lived.

1

If our dating of his book is correct, he is probably the same Obadiah mentioned in 2 Chronicles 17:7. There we are told that Jehoshaphat, king of Judah (873–848 B.C.) and the father of Jehoram, sent Obadiah along with other officials to revive the true worship in the land by instructing the people in the Book of the Law of the Lord. This would make Obadiah a contemporary of Elijah and Elisha, who were non-writing prophets in Israel at that time.

The Scriptures do not say or suggest any more than this about Obadiah, a prophet in Judah. If nothing else, the obscurity of his background encourages us to concentrate on his message.

Date

The date when Obadiah wrote his prophecy must be linked to the event referred to in verses 11-14, an attack upon Jerusalem. During this event the Edomites, Israel's neighbors to the south, had a hand in the shameful abuse of the Jewish capital and its inhabitants.

An event like this occurred in 586 B.C. That is the year when King Nebuchadnezzar and the Babylonians captured Jerusalem (2 Kings 25:1-21; 2 Chronicles 36:15-20; Jeremiah 52:1-30). Psalm 137 records how the Edomites eagerly encouraged the Babylonians to destroy the city down to its very foundations.

It does not seem likely, however, that Obadiah was referring to this attack on Jerusalem. If he had been an eyewitness, why didn't he report how the city and its magnificent temple had been totally destroyed, how the temple articles and the people were carried off into exile in Babylon? He makes no mention of this horrible devastation of the Holy City.

Second Chronicles 21:16,17 records an attack upon Jerusalem that is more likely the reference Obadiah has in mind. During the time of Jehoram, king of Judah from 848 to 841 B.C., the Philistines and Arabians attacked Jerusalem, taking both plunder and captives. This invasion of the Holy City occurred shortly after Jehoram unsuccessfully tried to put down a revolt by the Edomites (verses 8-10). As a result, the Edomites remained hostile toward the Israelites.

Accordingly, we accept the year 845 B.C. as the approximate date when Obadiah wrote his book, and we see in it a double fulfillment or reference. The immediate reference is to the invasion of Jerusalem by the Philistines and Arabians at the time of King Jehoram. Obadiah's prophecy was fulfilled again at the time the Babylonians destroyed Jerusalem some 250 years later, as Obadiah's predictive words in verses 11-14 seem to indicate.

Purpose and message

The people of Edom were lifelong enemies of the Israelites. The Edomites were like a thorn in the flesh as they seized every opportunity to cause Israel trouble. Finally Edom's cup of iniquity was full to the brim, and God stepped in with judgment. Obadiah correctly declared God's judgment that Edom would be attacked and destroyed. But there was hope for the remnant of Israel and for any penitent Edomite on "the day of the LORD" (verse 15) when God would provide deliverance on Mount Zion (verse 17)—a direct reference to the redemptive work of the Messiah.

The message of Obadiah, then, is basically one of divine retribution and restoration, centering around the theme of God's judgment on a proud and rebellious people, the Edomites.

3

Outline

Theme: God's judgment on Edom

    I. The destruction of Edom predicted (1-9)

   II. The cause of Edom's punishment (10-14)

  III. The day of the Lord: retribution and restoration (15-21)

PART ONE

The Destruction of Edom Predicted
(1-9)

The Lord will send nations to attack Edom

¹The vision of Obadiah.

This is what the Sovereign LORD says about Edom—

> **We have heard a message from the Lord:**
> **An envoy was sent to the nations to say,**
> **"Rise, and let us go against her for battle"—**

> **² "See, I will make you small among the nations;**
> **you will be utterly despised.**

With his opening words Obadiah establishes his credentials as a spokesman for the Lord. His term "vision" is equivalent to the word of the Lord, as 1 Samuel 3:1 makes clear: "In those days the word of the LORD was rare; there were not many visions." The other writing prophets also use the term *vision,* or *oracle,* or simply state that the word of the Lord came to them. In every case, they are stating clearly and emphatically that what they are about to declare is not the result of their own keen insights or perceptive understanding of God's Word. Rather, it is a divine communication, given to them to reveal the Lord's will.

Obadiah's next words make this truth abundantly clear. "This is what the Sovereign LORD says." Here we have the standard Old Testament formula for divine declarations, much like Jesus' New Testament assertion, "I tell you the truth" (Matthew 5:18), or in the words of the King James Version, "Verily I say unto you." It has been estimated that phrases such as "so the Lord says" and "the word of the Lord came to" occur over 2,400 times in the Old Testament—about 1,300 times in the prophetic books alone. What convincing support for the doctrine of the verbal inspiration of the Scriptures!

Esau and the Edomites

The Lord's revelation to Obadiah also made clear the purpose of that revelation, to declare "what the Sovereign LORD says about Edom." Edom and the Edomites were descendants of Esau, a son of Isaac and grandson of Abraham. He had received the name Edom when he said to his twin brother, Jacob, "'Quick, let me have some of that red stew! I'm famished!' (That is why he was also called Edom)" (Genesis 25:30). In Hebrew, Edom means "red" and refers to the red lentil stew as well as to Esau's red hair (verse 25). A brief account of Esau and his descendants is given in Genesis chapter 36.

Reminiscent of action taken by Abraham and his nephew Lot, Esau separated himself from Jacob when their cattle became too numerous for the land to support. He and his wives and children then settled south of Moab and the Dead Sea in the hill country of Seir after he had driven out the Horites, the original cave-dwelling inhabitants of the land. The country became known as Edom, and its inhabitants developed into a well-organized nation governed by kings before Israel had any king of its own.

The reason for the Lord's message concerning Edom is that her cup of iniquity was full to the brim. The Lord had a strong case against Edom because of her defiant pride in regard to him and because of her cruel hostility toward the Israelites, the descendants of Esau's twin brother, Jacob.

When Obadiah says "We have heard a message from the LORD," he is using the "editorial we" writers like to use to keep their person in the background. This seems typical of Obadiah, who is more concerned about the Lord's message than he is about himself.

We have no record of any "envoy," or messenger, sent by the Lord to rouse nations in judgment against Edom. But in one way or another, God, the ruler of all nations and peoples, directed countries and peoples like Syria, Babylon, Persia, the Nabataeans and, some time later, Rome to raise the war cry against Edom: "Rise, and let us go against her for battle." They would become instruments in God's hand to carry out his will. And isn't this the way God has always used nations and their courses in the world, to carry out his will and promote his plan of salvation? Truly all of history is *his* story!

Speaking through the prophet Obadiah, the Lord warns the descendants of Esau that he will use the nations he has roused to action to make Edom small and despised on the face of the earth. Edom never was a great nation to begin with. What prominence the nation had was a result of Edom's mineral resources and strategic location, straddling the King's Highway, an important caravan route. But when the Lord was through with it, whatever status Edom once had among the nations would be gone. The entire 35th chapter of Ezekiel expands upon this thought.

> [3] **The pride of your heart has deceived you,**
> **you who live in the clefts of the rocks**
> **and make your home on the heights,**
> **you who say to yourself,**
> **'Who can bring me down to the ground?'**
> [4] **Though you soar like the eagle**
> **and make your nest among the stars,**
> **from there I will bring you down,"**
>
> **declares the LORD.**

The reference to "the pride of your heart" points to the chief sin of the Edomites, the sinful pride of self-exaltation and arrogant self-confidence. They took an undue pride in their isolation and defensible position in Sela (verses 3,4), their treasures and wealth (verses 5,6), their political and military allies (verse 7), and their vaunted wisdom (verse 8).

Edom and Sela

Humanly speaking, Edom had cause to boast about its geographical location. The country of Edom was located directly south of the Dead Sea, straddling the Wadi Arabah, the deep rift that runs from the Dead Sea south to the Gulf of Aqaba. At times Edom's shifting borders reached the full 100 miles to the Gulf of Aqaba, but they seldom were more than 50 miles wide at any point in its history. It was situated on the plateau of Mount Seir, 5,000 feet above sea level, and boasted two chief cities: Bozrah to the north, with its almost impregnable fortress, and Teman (present-day Tawilan) in the center, protected by the fortress at nearby Sela.

The 19th-century English poet John William Burgon described the city of Sela (today known as Petra) with a phrase of enduring charm, calling it "a rose-red city, half as old as time." Indeed, the only entrance to Sela is through a long gorge of unbelievable beauty. With a small stream flowing along its floor, this canyon, or *siq* as the Arabs call it, snakes its way along for over a mile before it reaches the city. Towering more than 200 feet on either side of the canyon are perpendicular and overhanging cliffs of reddish-colored sandstone—hence its name Edom, "red." At places the gorge is only 12 feet in width, making it possible for a handful of men to hold off an invading army. This feature made Edom's inhabitants feel secure against the enemy. So did their "home on the heights," for they lived "in the clefts

Siq—Petra's entrance

of the rocks." The word "rocks" could be translated as *sela*, the Hebrew word for "rock." At least 60 of the cave dwellings in the high cliffs of Sela still remain in this city, which the Nabataeans later called Petra (Greek for "rock").

It was the rugged inaccessibility of this mountain fortress that gave the Edomites a false sense of security. "Who can bring me down to the ground?" they boasted, as if to say, "What enemy can launch a successful attack against us? Let them try!" But their sinful pride and defiant arrogance had given them the same short-sightedness of all who suffer from an inflated opinion of themselves. By not looking beyond the nose of their own pride, they failed to see the One against whom no fortress is impregnable and from whom no one can hide. David stated it so clearly when he wrote in Psalm 139,

> Where can I flee from your presence?
> If I go up to the heavens, you are there;
> if I make my bed in the depths, you are there.
>
> (verses 7,8)

The Lord's answer to Edom's swaggering pride and boastful claim is a literary gem. "Though you soar like the eagle and make your nest among the stars" refers to their protected homes in the high mountains of Edom. It could also refer symbolically to the height of pride on which the Edomites had placed themselves. There are also those who feel it has reference to the corrupt religion of the Edomites, who had deified Esau and used the eagle to represent him as their god.

" 'Though you soar like the eagle and make your nest among the stars, from there I will bring you down,' declares the LORD." Edom's days are numbered, and her destiny is doom and destruction at the hands of the nations chosen by the Lord. Has any nation or person ever won a battle against the Lord? Can the will of the Almighty successfully be thwarted by the power, cunning, and defiance of mortal, sinful man? Even though the patriarch Jacob did prevail over God at Peniel (Genesis 32) and was therefore called Israel ("he struggles with God"), yet God let him know who was in control by striking his hip socket so he became lame. Jacob prevailed in prayer for the Lord's blessing only because the Lord permitted him to do so. But out-duel the Lord? Never, for no one is the Lord's lord!

Edom will be completely destroyed

> [5] "If thieves came to you,
>   if robbers in the night—
> Oh, what a disaster awaits you—
>   would they not steal only as much as they wanted?
> If grape pickers came to you,
>   would they not leave a few grapes?
> [6] But how Esau will be ransacked,
>   his hidden treasures pillaged!
> [7] All your allies will force you to the border;
>   your friends will deceive and overpower you;
> those who eat your bread will set a trap for you,
>   but you will not detect it.

In the preceding verses the Lord spoke to Edom on the matter of the arrogant pride she had taken in her isolated and defensible location among the high cliffs of Sela. But the Lord's hand of judgment would tumble Edom from her heights. Now the Lord addresses Edom on the pride she had placed in her wealth and in the power and security she felt her wealth could buy.

It might seem that a thirsty desert land south of the Dead Sea would have had little wealth to brag about. But there were several factors that contributed to Edom's prosperity.

11

For one thing, copper and iron deposits were found in the Arabah. After smelting the ore at their southernmost city, Ezion Geber, the Edomites engaged in a lively and profitable business of exporting these precious metals.

A second factor brought even greater wealth. Running right through the middle of Edom was the King's Highway, the main north-south trade route east of the Jordan River. As a look at the map on page 29 will show, the King's Highway connected with trade routes to Egypt and Africa, and to Arabia and India. All along this route were tax offices, ready to demand custom duties and tolls from the frequent camel and donkey caravans carrying gold, silver, spices, and fine clothing. In addition, the King's Highway passed through the narrow gorge leading to the fortress city of Sela. This unique position allowed the Edomites to control virtually all travel along the trade route. The Edomites had wealth, and they felt secure in their wealth—boastfully secure.

Isn't that how the foolish rich man in Jesus' parable felt (Luke 12:16-21)? With his barns filled to overflowing, he felt confident that he could get along without God. Doesn't the same temptation face each of us as the Lord permits us to acquire more of the material goods of this world? Daily we need to pray, "Lord, do not allow my sinful pride to place your earthly blessings between you and me!"

Edom's pride in her wealth would give her no security before God. For when God would send his appointed nations to bring judgment upon Edom, all her wealth would do her no good. In fact, she would lose it. "How Esau [or Edom] will be ransacked!" Not like thieves and robbers who "steal only as much as they [want]," nor like grape pickers, who don't search under every leaf but always "leave a few grapes" when they harvest—no, the plundering nations would strip Edom of all its wealth: even "hidden treasures" would be "pillaged."

The nations surrounding Edom had recognized her prosperous position of trade and power and were eager to gain and retain the goodwill of the nation that controlled their lifeline. Therefore Edom had political friends and military allies in the Arabians, the Moabites, and the Ammonites to the north and east. Edom carried on slave trade with Gaza and Tyre, cities along the Mediterranean coast. Edom took great pride in the security these allies afforded.

Yet at the time of God's judgment, this source of pride would desert Edom. "All your allies [literally 'men of your covenant'] will force you to the border," driving her out and taking over her country, as the Arab tribe of Nabataeans did in 325 B.C. These political friends had deceived Edom by secretly plotting against her while peacefully eating "bread" at her table. The trap was set for Edom's downfall by the deception of her allies, who not only deserted Edom when she was attacked but also helped to overpower her. Their deception was clever. "You will not detect it."

When Edom lost her wealth, she also lost her attractiveness to other nations and thus lost her effective power. She had sought strength and security in her strategic position and in her allies, but she left the Lord out of her planning. That spelled her doom. The words of Solomon in Psalm 127 apply to nations as well as to individuals: "Unless the LORD builds the house, its builders labor in vain" (verse 1). Psalm 33 supports this truth by saying, "Blessed is the nation whose God is the LORD" (verse 12), and then goes on to declare that no nation is saved by the size and strength of its military machine. What a lesson for the nations of today, including our own!

Economic pacts, arms limitation agreements, shuttle diplomacy, and summit meetings by heads of state can only produce a temporary, fragile state of peace. Unless these efforts are undertaken in the fear of the Lord and seek his help and guidance, they are wasted.

> **⁸ "In that day," declares the LORD,**
> **"will I not destroy the wise men of Edom,**
> **men of understanding in the mountains of Esau?**
> **⁹ Your warriors, O Teman, will be terrified,**
> **and everyone in Esau's mountains**
> **will be cut down in the slaughter.**

Here the Lord is referring to the wisdom for which Edom was famous. The mention of Teman in verse 9 suggests that the book of Job may have come out of an Edomite background. Eliphaz, one of the friends of Job who came to comfort him, was a Temanite (Job 2:11). Whatever their wisdom—financial, political, military, practical—the Edomites took great pride in it, but all in vain. "In that day," the day when God would judge their sin, when friend and ally would desert Edom and turn against her, the Edomites would need wise and intelligent leadership more than ever. But "your warriors, O Teman, will be terrified," panic-stricken because they will have no knowledge or wisdom of what to do and where to flee. The city of Teman, located near Sela in eastern Edom, received its name from Esau's grandson by the same name (Genesis 36:15) and is used here to represent Edom.

The Lord's judgment upon Edom will be complete: "Everyone in Esau's mountains will be cut down in the slaughter." Obadiah will have more to say on this later.

PART TWO

The Cause of Edom's Punishment

(10-14)

Edom showed hostility toward Judah, God's covenant people

¹⁰ Because of the violence against your brother Jacob,
you will be covered with shame;
you will be destroyed forever.
¹¹ On the day you stood aloof
while strangers carried off his wealth
and foreigners entered his gates
and cast lots for Jerusalem,
you were like one of them.

Nestled high among the cliffs of inaccessible Sela and growing rich and powerful through trade and commerce, Edom prided herself in her security against all forces, including the Lord. This defiant pride showed itself in Edom's hostility toward the Lord's chosen people, Judah.

Esau and Jacob

Obadiah's reference to Edom's "violence against your brother Jacob" reminds us of the bad blood that Esau had for Jacob from the very beginning. While the twins were still in their mother's womb, "the babies jostled each other" (Genesis 25:22), and the Lord told her what this meant. Her two sons would become two separate nations, the younger being the stronger and ruling over the older. Esau selfishly and foolishly despised the privileges of his birthright, thereby forfeiting the power and ruling rank his position as the older brother would normally have entitled him to.

When Isaac blessed Jacob, he confirmed this subordinate role for Esau. And when he finally pronounced a blessing on Esau too, he spelled it out more clearly. Esau would live in a desert region "away from the earth's richness, away from the dew of heaven above" (27:39). He would live as a hostile nation in subjection to his brother Jacob but in the end would throw off this yoke of subjection (verse 40).

The cause of Esau's second-rate position over against Jacob was not God's idea. Esau had brought it on himself. His life demonstrated a consistent pattern of shameful neglect for the things of God and a determined defiance of God's will. Against the wishes of his parents and of God, Esau had married heathen wives. He continued to hold a murderous grudge against his twin brother, Jacob, who received the blessing of the firstborn. This "godless" son of Isaac and Rebekah, as Hebrews 12:16 describes him, had little love for his brother, Jacob, the bearer of the messianic promise.

Esau's descendants, the Edomites, were no better. When Jacob's descendants, the Israelites, were en route from Egypt to Canaan, Moses requested safe passage for Israel through the land of Edom. The Edomites gave their answer with raised swords barring the way (Numbers 20:14-21). Later they fought with Israel's King Saul and again with King David. He, however, broke Edom's power, placed military garrisons throughout the land, and exacted tribute from the Edomites (2 Samuel 8:11-14).

Edom raised its sword against Israel once more, this time against King Solomon. But he squashed the rebellion and occupied the Edomite cities of Ezion Geber and Elath on the Gulf of Aqaba as his seaports (1 Kings 11; 2 Chronicles 8). Edom was finally able to throw off Israel's domination when it successfully revolted against King Jehoram of Judah and gained its independence in 846 B.C. (2 Kings 8:20-22).

That Edom should display a hostile attitude toward anyone is bad enough, but against Judah, her brother nation and the covenant people of the Lord! What could be worse? Hatred for God's people is hatred for God himself. Therefore, Obadiah declared, "You will be covered with shame; you will be destroyed forever."

Jerusalem attacked

Then the day came in 845 B.C. when Judah was invaded by the Philistines and Arabs (2 Chronicles 21:16,17). They attacked Jerusalem, plundering the palace of its royal treasure and taking captives even from the king's family. Obadiah writes as an eyewitness. Listen to him accuse the Edomites: "You stood aloof while strangers carried off his wealth and foreigners entered his gates." The Edomites, blood brothers of the Israelites, did not raise a voice in protest or lift a finger to help the Jews while Jerusalem was being sacked. In fact, they did quite the opposite. The Edomites became "like one of them," even entering the city and joining the enemy when they "cast lots" to apportion Jerusalem and its inhabitants for plunder.

Edom gloated over the calamity of Judah

¹² **You should not look down on your brother**
in the day of his misfortune,
nor rejoice over the people of Judah
in the day of their destruction,
nor boast so much
in the day of their trouble.
¹³ **You should not march through the gates of my people**
in the day of their disaster,
nor look down on them in their calamity

in the day of their disaster,
nor seize their wealth
in the day of their disaster.
¹⁴ You should not wait at the crossroads
to cut down their fugitives,
nor hand over their survivors
in the day of their trouble.

As Obadiah reflects upon the sinful behavior of Edom during the attack on Jerusalem, he sees only evidence of her sin of pride. Rather than hiding her eyes in sympathetic horror, Edom looked down on Israel "in the day of his misfortune." Here was Edom *gloating* in pride over her brother's affliction. Edom displayed *malice* when she rejoiced "over the people of Judah in the day of their destruction." And what was it but *arrogance* when the Edomites hurled ridicule and biting insults at the Jerusalemites "in the day of their trouble"?

The Edomites were not content to view the agonizing destruction of Jerusalem from a distance. They displayed the *presumption* of marching right "through the gates" of the city to be front-row eyewitnesses on the scene of the "disaster." And then their sin against the inhabitants of Jerusalem took on an even more active nature. They began to seize the Israelites' wealth, in *greed* helping themselves to the spoils of sacked Jerusalem like hyenas feeding on another's kill. This scene is repeated in our day when looters swarm over a city devastated by a tornado or hurricane.

The climax of Edom's hostility toward Judah came when the Edomites *persecuted* the helpless refugees from Jerusalem. Like hungry lions, they waited "at the crossroads" leading out of the city and "cut down" the fugitives to prevent escape. Others were handed over bodily to their captors to be murdered or perhaps sold into slavery, for Edom had been engaged in this practice (Amos 1:6; Joel 3:3).

Each of the verbs in verses 12 to 14 contains "you should not," a condemnation of Edom's past behavior at the destruction of Jerusalem in 845 B.C. as well as a warning against repeating her sins in the future. This warning was still in place almost 260 years later, in 586 B.C., when Jerusalem was again attacked, this time by Babylon's King Nebuchadnezzar. He destroyed the city and its temple and deported most of the inhabitants into exile in Babylon, a thousand miles from Jerusalem. Edom's treacherous role in this destruction is denounced in Psalm 137, which was written after the exile:

> Remember, O LORD, what the Edomites did
>   on the day Jerusalem fell.
> "Tear it down," they cried,
>   "tear it down to its foundations!" (verse 7)

Pride

"You should not have done this, Edom! You should not do it again!" Through Obadiah, God could only condemn Edom's sin of pride and warn against repeating it, because pride is the sin of sins. It was the first sin, the sin that caused the fall of Satan. Isaiah describes Satan's pride vividly when he quotes the devil, "I will raise my throne above the stars of God. . . . I will make myself like the Most High" (Isaiah 14:13,14).

Pride seeks to dethrone God by elevating the sinner to a position equal to or above that of God. Pride cheats God by taking credit due him. Defiantly it claims that humans can live without any help from the almighty God. It refuses to take God into account in planning for life. Pride insults God by arrogantly claiming, "I am the master of my fate; I am the captain of my soul."

The offspring pride bears are sins against God and one's neighbor: presumption, malice, boasting, greed, murder, persecution, slander. In fact, most sins can be traced back to the parent sin of pride. The prevalent "I and mine are first" attitude comes from pride. So does secularism, with its emphasis on living without religion.

Pride is so commonplace that the psalmist says people wear it like a necklace (Psalm 73:6). And it is deceptive, as the Lord reminded Edom, "The pride of your heart has deceived you" (Obadiah 3). How easy it is for Christians also to fall into the sin of pride! We have only to leave God out of our planning and to slip into the habit of neglecting the Bible and prayer, and we too will fall into the sinful practice of living our lives on a secular basis, not giving God and his will first place.

A careful reading of Psalm 10 will sharpen our awareness of the sin of pride and its ugly consequences. And then our penitent hearts will be eager to seek forgiveness from the Lord, who "opposes the proud but gives grace to the humble" (1 Peter 5:5).

PART THREE

The Day of the Lord: Retribution and Restoration
(15-21)

Edom will be fully punished for her sins

¹⁵ "The day of the LORD is near
 for all nations.
As you have done, it will be done to you;
 your deeds will return upon your own head.
¹⁶ Just as you drank on my holy hill,
 so all the nations will drink continually;
they will drink and drink
 and be as if they had never been.

Obadiah has saved the best for last. His prophecy now points to "the day of the LORD." Obadiah is the first of the literary prophets to use this term, which occurs more than 140 times in the Old Testament.

There is a good deal of variety in the ways in which the term "the day of the LORD" is put to use. It may refer to the establishment of the church (Isaiah 2), to the defeat of Babylon (Isaiah 13), or to the destruction caused by a plague of locusts (Joel 2). In a narrower sense one might even speak of "the day of the LORD" as the time when he intervenes in people's lives with sickness, disaster, or even death. In each case, however, the term refers to a time when God carries out his will—either in judgment or redemption.

One more thing must be said. All the days of the LORD point to the one great and last "day of the LORD." On that day the Son of God will come in final judgment on his unbelieving enemies as well as for the eternal deliverance of his faithful followers (Matthew 24,25). Whenever God lifts his hand in judgment upon individuals and nations during this present age, he is giving us an urgent warning to repent before his final judgment and to turn in faith to the Savior for forgiveness.

"The day of the LORD" therefore is messianic in its final point of reference. Obadiah has that in mind also, even though his immediate reference here is to the temporal fate of Edom. Her day of retribution was "near" because God's judgment does not hover over nations forever. His bills may not all come due quickly, but they come due. Saint Peter says, "With the Lord a day is like a thousand years, and a thousand years are like a day" (2 Peter 3:8). And the apostle Paul reminds us, "A man reaps what he sows" (Galatians 6:7).

As Edom had rejected the Lord and despised and mistreated his covenant people, so "it will be done" to her. God would reject and punish her fully, as he in fact does with all nations who continue in their sins. In Old Testament prophecy, Edom was often emblematic of world powers hostile to God. God's judgment on Edom anticipates his complete removal of all who oppose him.

"Just as you drank on my holy hill" may refer to an actual act of drunken debauchery the Edomites committed on Mount Zion, the temple mount, when they marched through the gates of Jerusalem (verse 13). Or Obadiah may be using this phrase figuratively to describe Edom's cruel and degrading treatment of God's chosen people.

Edom and all nations who defy the Lord "will drink and drink" of the Lord's cup of wrath and judgment until they will "be as if they had never been." The prophet Jeremiah describes in vivid detail the fatal consequences for Edom and the nations when they must drink of God's cup of wrath: "Drink, get drunk and vomit, and fall to rise no more because of the sword I will send among you" (Jeremiah 25:27).

Is there, then, no escape from God's judgment? Yes, "on Mount Zion will be deliverance" (Obadiah 17), even for wicked Edom if she repents.

Israel will be graciously restored

> [17] But on Mount Zion will be deliverance;
> it will be holy,
> and the house of Jacob
> will possess its inheritance.
> [18] The house of Jacob will be a fire
> and the house of Joseph a flame;
> the house of Esau will be stubble,
> and they will set it on fire and consume it.
> There will be no survivors
> from the house of Esau."
>
> **The LORD has spoken.**

On the northern hill of ancient Jerusalem was a promontory called Moriah, or Mount Zion. It was here that King Solomon built his magnificent temple. When the Lord's glory filled the temple at its dedication (1 Kings 8:10,11), that building represented the visible place of his dwelling among Israel. Zion became the heart of Jerusalem, of all Israel, of the church of God in the Old Testament. Fittingly, it is also used as a symbol of the New Testament church, the heavenly Jerusalem (Hebrews 12:22). On this Mount Zion will be a "holy" deliverance. This is the saving holiness, or righteousness, of Jesus Christ that the church offers to one and all as it proclaims the gospel.

Stated another way, "the house of Jacob will possess its inheritance." The house of Jacob is the spiritual house of

Jacob, the New Testament church (Luke 1:33). Its inheritance contains the means of grace and all the spiritual blessings they supply: faith, forgiveness, hope, comfort, strength, life, eternal salvation.

But the church's inheritance also includes all the elect of God, those predestined to salvation, who come to faith by the preaching of the gospel. Again, there is hope for wicked Edom if she repents.

But if not, the house of Jacob and the house of Joseph will destroy Edom like a flaming fire torching dry stubble. Manasseh and Ephraim, the two sons born to Joseph in Egypt, were allotted land in Palestine in place of Joseph. They became the strongest of the ten northern tribes of Israel. At times their names or that of their father Joseph stood for the entire Northern Kingdom. Here Obadiah predicts the reunion of the Southern Kingdom of Judah and the Northern Kingdom of Israel, divided since 931 B.C. This reunion took place after the Babylonian exiles returned to Palestine.

The Idumeans

Together Judah and Israel will bring God's judgment to bear upon Edom until "there will be no survivors." History records that this very thing happened to the Edomites. Around 435 B.C. the Arab tribe of Nabataeans captured Sela and drove the Edomites out, forcing them to migrate to the barren Negev, the hot, dry southland of Judah. Now called Idumeans (Greek for Edomites, Mark 3:8), they harassed Judah until the Jewish leader Judas Maccabaeus defeated them in 185 B.C. in a bloody struggle that cost the lives of 20,000 Idumeans. Some 50 years later, another of the ruling Maccabees, John Hyrcanus, forced Judaism upon the Idumeans by compelling them to accept Jewish laws, including circumcision. For a time this worked in their favor because under the Romans, who conquered Palestine in 64 B.C., some Idumeans rose to local power. There was Antipater, appointed procurator, or governor, of Judea. His son, Herod the Great, the butcher of Bethlehem, became king of Judea. Herod Antipas, the king who beheaded John the Baptist, served as ruler of Galilee. Herod Agrippa I was king of Palestine when he killed the apostle James and imprisoned Peter.

This infamous claim to power, however, was short-lived. The Idumeans joined the Jews in revolting against the Romans in A.D. 70. Emperor Titus destroyed not only Jerusalem but most of the Idumeans as well. The few survivors were absorbed by other tribes. So the once proud nation of Edom, secure in its heights and trusting in its wealth, was no more. And isn't this exactly what the Lord had predicted? "I will make you small among the nations" (verse 2); "I will bring you down" (verse 4); "Everyone . . . will be cut down in the slaughter" (verse 9).

> ¹⁹ **People from the Negev will occupy**
> **the mountains of Esau,**
> **and people from the foothills will possess**
> **the land of the Philistines.**
> **They will occupy the fields of Ephraim and Samaria,**
> **and Benjamin will possess Gilead.**
> ²⁰ **This company of Israelite exiles who are in Canaan**
> **will possess the land as far as Zarephath;**
> **the exiles from Jerusalem who are in Sepharad**
> **will possess the towns of the Negev.**

There will be a restoration of Israel. The Jews who were scattered by their enemies (often with the aid of the Edomites) will return to reclaim their land. They will come from the Negev, or south land, and from the western foothills, or

25

Shephelah. Exiles will come from Canaan, here meaning the land of Phoenicia (present-day Lebanon), with Zarephath midway between Tyre and Sidon. Exiles will also come from Sepharad. Its exact location is unknown, but the most likely identification is Sardis, not far from Ephesus in southwest Asia Minor.

How are we to understand the fulfillment of these words of restoration? Did the Lord mean the Jews were to repossess their land for all time, that they would be restored as a nation to reestablish the earthly kingdom of David? There are some Bible scholars who interpret it this way. As proof they point to the establishment of the State of Israel in 1948, supported by the Zionist movement. They look for this restored nation to continue to grow and prosper and become a world power.

To be sure, the Lord did mean that the Jews scattered by wars and exiled by the Babylonians would return to reclaim their land, as he had promised (Deuteronomy 30:1-5). The Lord kept his promise when in 536 B.C. the exiles began to return from Babylon under Ezra the scribe.

But earthly restoration was not the complete fulfillment of this prophecy. The prophecy looks to a spiritual restoration and possession fulfilled in the promised Messiah. Balaam prophesied in Numbers 24:17,18 that "a star will come out of Jacob; a scepter will rise out of Israel. . . . Edom will be conquered; Seir, his enemy, will be conquered." The star and the scepter is the Messiah and his saving power, who came from the line of Jacob, the chosen family. Under Christ, the Messiah, Edom would be possessed. Through the prophet Amos, the Lord promised to "restore David's fallen tent . . . so that they may possess the remnant of Edom and all the nations that bear my name" (9:11,12). Again, this is a reference to a spiritual possessing by the house of David through the messianic line from Jacob.

Accordingly, the complete fulfillment of Obadiah's prophecy is to be found in the messianic era. The restoration that the Lord promises is the gathering of all believers in Jesus Christ into the latter-day Israel, the New Testament church. By preaching the gospel of Jesus Christ, this spiritual house of Jacob possesses Jew and Gentile alike for the Savior and adds them to the church. In Ephesians 3:6 the apostle Paul states the principle, "Through the gospel the Gentiles are heirs together with Israel, members together of one body, and sharers together in the promise in Christ Jesus."

The day of the Lord is upon us! He is restoring his spiritual Israel by means of the gospel. This means each believer is involved, for Obadiah is referring to evangelism. He makes this especially clear in the last verse of his prophecy.

> **21 Deliverers will go up on Mount Zion**
> **to govern the mountains of Esau.**
> **And the kingdom will be the LORD's.**

The word "deliverers" is also used for the judges, like Deborah, Gideon, and Samson. They carried out God's judgment by delivering Israel from the oppression of her enemies. The deliverers Obadiah has in mind are those who bring deliverance from the slavery of sin and the power of the devil. He is referring to the messengers of the gospel, who by their preaching and witnessing are to be

> a light for the Gentiles,
> to open eyes that are blind,
> to free captives from prison
> and to release from the dungeon those who
> sit in darkness. (Isaiah 42:6,7)

These gospel messengers will go "on"—or, as the NIV footnote reads, "from"—Mount Zion, the New Testament church. They will go "to govern the mountains of Esau," that is, to lead the descendants of Esau, the Edomites, out of the oppression of their sin into the glorious salvation to be found in the Savior Jesus Christ.

All unbelievers are Edomites, spiritual Edomites, who by their sinful pride and unbelief have opposed the will of God and despised his people. Yet, God loves them and gave his Son into death for their sins, as well as for the sins of others. He does not want "anyone to perish, but everyone to come to repentance" (2 Peter 3:9). We who belong to the spiritual house of Jacob have a job to do, an exciting job and a privilege. God calls upon us to bring the gospel to the unbelievers, to show them the way to their Savior, Jesus Christ.

"And the kingdom will be the LORD's." The Lord rules by his gospel in the hearts and lives of all believers. On the last great day of the Lord, he will rule with all his redeemed in the eternity of heaven. Then the gracious restoration of God's people will be complete.

What a beautiful note of triumph on which Obadiah's prophecy comes to a close! None of the prophets has a more exalted climax. Obadiah seems to be looking ahead to Revelation 11:15:

> The kingdom of the world has become the
> kingdom of our Lord and of his Christ,
> and he will reign for ever and ever.

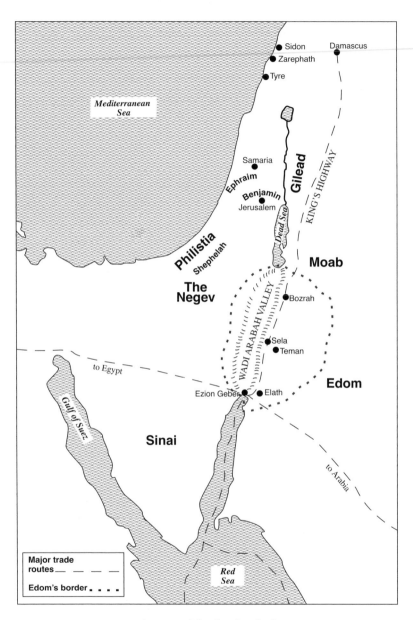

The world of Obadiah

INTRODUCTION TO JONAH

The book of Jonah is listed fifth among the 12 so-called minor prophets, the shorter prophetic books of the Old Testament. Yet the book contains less prophecy than any of the others. Only one brief sentence of five words in the original Hebrew can be called an actual prophecy: "Forty more days and Nineveh will be overturned" (3:4). The rest of the book is largely biographical, narrating how the prophet Jonah carried out his Lord's commission to preach to the Ninevites.

The prophetic message, however, lies not only in what Jonah said to Nineveh, but also in what God said and did to Jonah in connection with his divine commission to that capital city of Assyria (present-day Iraq and part of Iran).

Many people know of the book of Jonah largely because of the narrative of "the whale" swallowing Jonah. This is unfortunate because the "whale," or great fish, appears in only one brief episode for a total of three verses (1:17; 2:1,10). And it is not the most important part of the Jonah narrative either.

Yet this account has caused Jonah to be one of the most—if not *the* most—misunderstood and challenged books of the Bible. The great fish swallowing Jonah and vomiting him up alive is a miracle many find hard to accept, along with the other miracles in the book. The entire book, then, is explained away as myth, folktale, allegory, parable, religious fiction, nonhistorical prose, or whatever.

The critics all miss the main point of the Jonah narrative. It is not about the great fish. And the story, strictly speaking, is not Jonah's story either. It is the story of God's compassionate dealing both with his servant Jonah and with the ancient heathen city of Nineveh. God is front and center on the stage of action. His word begins the story, "The word of the LORD came to Jonah" (1:1), and his question ends it, "Should I not be concerned about that great city?" (4:11).

And Jonah? He is to be commended for his prayer in chapter 2. And he did go to Nineveh after his second commissioning, although reluctantly. For the most part, however, he was acting the part of a spoiled and self-centered child: begrudging, disobeying, running away, pouting.

The book of Jonah, then, is God's story. We will want to keep this in mind as we study the book.

Author

The author is not mentioned in the book or anywhere else in Scripture. Critical scholars claim the author wrote it centuries after Jonah's time. Most conservative scholars, however, ascribe the book to Jonah. The intense personal prayer from the belly of the fish could be known only by the one who spoke it. And who but the author himself would be able to give penetrating insights into his own character, to confess his own disobedience and failures, to portray so vividly the unforgettable lesson God taught him, and then be willing to put it down in writing? We do not hesitate to accept Jonah as the author of the book.

Apart from what the book itself tells us, the only known facts of Jonah's life are recorded in 2 Kings 14:25, which tells how Israel's King Jeroboam II restored the borders of Israel "in accordance with the word of the LORD, the God of Israel, spoken through his servant Jonah son of Amittai, the prophet from Gath Hepher."

The Hebrew name Jonah means "dove," and Amittai, "truthful." Could both names be significant in view of Jonah's commission to represent Israel (called a "dove" in Hosea 7:11 and Psalm 74:19) in bringing the truthful message of God's love to Nineveh? Perhaps. At any rate, we know something about his hometown, Gath Hepher. It was located on the eastern border of the territory of Zebulun in northern Israel (Joshua 19:13), on a small hill about three miles northeast of Nazareth.

Jonah was therefore a Galilean prophet of the Northern Kingdom of Israel. When he went to Nineveh, he became the first apostle sent to the Gentiles. This makes his book the earliest and, with the exception of the book of Acts, the greatest of missionary books.

Date

Again our source is 2 Kings 14:25. Jonah was active before and during the reign of Jeroboam II, king of Israel from 793 B.C. to 753 B.C. Jonah may have written his book shortly after he returned from Nineveh, about 780 B.C. A date such as this has long been accepted by both the ancient Jewish church and the early Christian church. Accordingly, Jonah lived about 80 years after Elisha and was an early contemporary of the prophets Amos (760 B.C.), Hosea (750 B.C.), Isaiah (740 B.C.), and Micah (730 B.C.).

Occasion and purpose

Jonah received his commission from the Lord at a unique time in Israel's history. The Northern Kingdom of Israel had been in a weakened condition. Her vile sinfulness and ill-advised political relations with her neighbors had diminished

Israel's fortunes considerably. In his famous Black Obelisk, the Assyrian king Shalmaneser III relates how he fought the bloody battle at Qarqar in Syria (853 B.C.) to put down a revolt by a number of Syrian kings joined by Ahab, king of Israel. Later Israel was forced to pay tribute to the same Assyrian king. In the meantime, Israel's own borders were shrinking as it lost possession of one after another of its outlying areas. And "everyone in Israel, whether slave or free, was suffering" (2 Kings 14:26).

At this low point in Israel's history, the Lord sent his prophet Jonah to King Jeroboam II with the promise of restoration and better days. Jeroboam reigned for 40 years as Israel's 13th king and became one of her most powerful kings. Yet, for all the prosperity and military power he enjoyed, he was a very evil king. "He did evil in the eyes of the LORD" (2 Kings 14:24).

It was no different with the people. Although they enjoyed outward prosperity, they lived in spiritual poverty. Through Jonah, the Lord had given his promise of restoration to encourage fallen Israel to repent of her evil and return to the goodness of the Lord. But the people did not use this time of grace. They not only failed to repent, they even increased in their wicked ways.

> They forsook all the commands of the LORD their God and made for themselves two idols cast in the shape of calves, and an Asherah pole. They bowed down to all the starry hosts, and they worshiped Baal. They sacrificed their sons and daughters in the fire. They practiced divination and sorcery and sold themselves to do evil in the eyes of the LORD, provoking him to anger. (2 Kings 17:16,17)

In his book the prophet Amos describes the luxurious living of the wealthy upper class and the accompanying social and moral corruption that prevailed in the land at this time.

Meanwhile, things in Assyria were going downhill. After years of conquest and prosperity, a general decline set in that lasted for almost half a century. The king was stripped of his power. High political and military officials ruled the empire, but they wasted the strength of Assyria in efforts to conquer western Asia Minor while neglecting affairs back home. Numerous revolts by the provinces also weakened the nation.

At this low point in Assyria's history, the Lord sent the prophet Jonah to Nineveh, Assyria's capital city. God's full reasons for doing this we will consider later, but let this reason be noted now: Jonah was to preach repentance to Nineveh so it might be saved from its own destruction long enough to be the scourge in God's hand to punish Israel with destruction!

Israel's destruction came in 722 B.C. when the Lord allowed Shalmaneser V of Assyria to attack and defeat the Northern Kingdom. He then deported its inhabitants to captivity and oblivion in Assyria.

In 612 B.C. Nineveh received its final judgment from God when it was destroyed by a military alliance of the Medes and Babylonians. The prophet Nahum uses his entire book to describe the deep moral corruption and wickedness of Nineveh and the destruction that followed.

Fact or fiction?

Jonah fits well into the history of Israel and Assyria. But not all people see it that way. Many critical scholars see in Jonah more fiction than fact. Consider the following:

> Surely this is not the record of actual historical events nor was it ever intended as such. It is a sin against the author to treat as literal prose what he intended as poetry. . . . His story is thus a story

with a moral, a parable, a prose poem like the story of the Good Samaritan. (Julius A. Bewer, "Jonah," *The International Critical Commentary*, page 4)

The Jerusalem Bible calls the story of Jonah a "droll adventure" and adds, "Though God is indeed master of nature, the successive prodigies here narrated read like a succession of practical jokes played by God on his prophet." Then it goes on, "This late date [after the Exile] is warning enough against any interpretation of the book as history" (page 1141).

The historicity of Jonah is challenged because the critics find too many elements in his story impossible to accept. All the miracles, Jonah's mission to a foreign city, his thanksgiving song in chapter 2, the size of Nineveh, the language Jonah spoke to the Ninevites—these are among the "problems" the critics find in Jonah.

The miracles, though, are the real problem for the critics, especially Jonah's survival in the belly of the great fish. There is also the storm at sea, the repentance of Nineveh's citizens, the vine that sprang up overnight, and more. The critic argues that the abundance of these miracles (some count as high as 12) and the incredible nature of some of them is just too much for human reason.

Well, all miracles are too much for human reason, or they wouldn't be divine miracles! God intends his miracles to be accepted by faith and not by sight, by faith in an almighty and gracious God whose Word is truthful from cover to cover.

As for incredibility, are the miracles in Jonah any more incredible than Israel's clothing and shoes not wearing out during 40 years in the wilderness (Deuteronomy 29:5)? than the manna every morning (Exodus 16:14-35)? than Peter walking on the water (Matthew 14:29) or Lazarus walking out of the grave after four days (John 11:17,44)?

Some critics who cannot read Jonah as factual history regard it as no more than a story or legend, like one of the Greek or Roman myths. Others interpret Jonah as a parable in which the characters exist not in real life but only for the purpose of telling a story to teach a truth—here that God's mercy is not restricted to the Jews. Then there are those who insist the story is pure allegory, in which the characters and events are symbolic, used to present a more significant meaning beneath the surface of the narrative. Thus, we are told Jonah represents Israel; Nineveh, the gentile world; and the great fish, the exile in Babylon.

There is nothing in the biblical account to suggest that we are to take the story of Jonah as anything but pure historical fact. While it must be granted there may be symbolic meaning in the narrative, yet the narrative remains historically true. This is how Jews and Christians had regarded the book until a century ago. We have no question about the historicity of Jonah, since our Lord himself spoke of Jonah and Jonah's mission to Nineveh as historical fact (Matthew 12:39-41; 16:4; Luke 11:29-32).

Message

The message of the book of Jonah will be presented during the exposition. Part Five will discuss it in greater depth.

Outline

Theme: Jonah's mission to Nineveh
  I. The Lord's first call and Jonah's refusal (1:1-16)
  II. The Lord's deliverance of Jonah at sea and Jonah's prayer (1:17–2:10)
  III. The Lord's second call and Nineveh's repentance (3:1-10)
  IV. Jonah's displeasure and the Lord's rebuke (4:1-11)
  V. The message of the book of Jonah

PART ONE

The Lord's First Call and Jonah's Refusal
(1:1-16)

The Lord calls Jonah

1 **The word of the LORD came to Jonah son of Amittai:** **²"Go to the great city of Nineveh and preach against it, because its wickedness has come up before me."**

Jonah begins his book in a straightforward manner, going right into his call from the LORD, Jehovah, Israel's covenant-God. It is important to note how he was called: directly by the Lord himself. This was also true of the other prophets in the Old Testament and of the apostles in the New Testament. Such a call is said to be an *immediate* call, one issued by the Lord in person without going through a human agency. Today the Lord calls pastors, teachers, and missionaries into his service *mediately,* that is, through the agency of his church acting in his name.

In either case, the call is always connected with the word of the Lord. That gives the call its authority. The Lord alone knows whom he wants to call, what the person is to do, and where he or she is to serve.

Jonah's call was to "go to the great city of Nineveh." One of the most ancient cities in the world, Nineveh was founded by Nimrod, the great-grandson of Noah, shortly after the flood (Genesis 10:9-12). It was located on the bank of the Tigris River some 220 miles north and a little west of Baghdad in present-day Iraq. For five hundred years, until 612 B.C., it served as one of the capital cities of the mighty Assyrian Empire.

Jonah was sent to Nineveh to "preach against it, because its wickedness has come up" before the Lord. Even the king of Nineveh had to admit things were bad when he urged the Ninevites to give up "their evil ways and their violence" (3:8). Assyria was especially noted for her violence and her heartless cruelty. The prophet Nahum calls Nineveh "the city of blood, full of lies" (Nahum 3:1), where people stumbled over corpses without number piled up in the streets. King Ashurnasipal was said to take great delight in the high mound of human heads he erected after his victories. Assyria also took slaves in battle and deported entire populations to distant lands (2 Kings 15:29).

Assyria took pride in her military conquests (Isaiah 10:12-19). But her chief wickedness in God's eyes had to be her abominable idolatry, giving herself and her substance over to the licentious worship of gods like Asshur, Anu, Bel, and Ishtar. Her continued rejection of the Lord, with its accompanying evil, rose up before him like dirty dishes piling up in the sink, until his forbearance wore out. As Nahum put it so well, "The LORD is slow to anger and great in power; the LORD will not leave the guilty unpunished" (Nahum 1:3).

The Lord called Jonah to preach against this wicked city with the stark message "Forty more days and Nineveh will be overturned" (3:4). Repent or else! Forty days was grace on the Lord's part.

We should keep in mind that Jonah had been called as a prophet *to the people of Israel.* For God suddenly to terminate this and call the man away from his ministry to the covenant people dare not be regarded lightly. At Jonah's time (and Elijah's and Elisha's) the covenant nation was, however, violating God's covenant, an activity that always brings the judgment of God. In response to Israel's rebellion, God called Jonah to minister to the Assyrian nation, the nation that would be God's instrument for pouring out his wrath on Israel. Jonah's very call, then, has overtones of judgment on Israel, as well as overtones of God's Savior-love for Assyria.

Jonah flees from the Lord

³**But Jonah ran away from the LORD and headed for Tarshish. He went down to Joppa, where he found a ship bound for that port. After paying the fare, he went aboard and sailed for Tarshish to flee from the LORD.**

Is that possible? A called servant of the Lord running away from him? Why did Jonah run away? Different reasons have been advanced. Some suggest Jonah fled because he was afraid to go in person and proclaim God's judgment upon the cruel and violent Ninevites. But Jonah was no man of fear. Neither the storm at sea nor the prospect of being thrown overboard to drown reduced him to panic.

Others claim Jonah was a proud prophet. According to this view, he fled because he wanted to avoid predicting Nineveh's destruction when in the end God's mercy would spare the city, thereby making Jonah's words a seemingly empty threat. A prophet must be accurate to be believed, right? Yet, Jonah does not at all come off in the narrative as proud.

Another explanation puts Jonah in a more favorable light. He wanted so much to see his wayward Israelites repent that he thought only God's stern and merciless judgment on Nineveh would move them to repentance. But Jonah never mentioned that reason when he criticized God for showing mercy to the Ninevites in 4:2: "That is why I was so quick to flee to Tarshish. I knew that you are a gracious and compassionate God, slow to anger and abounding in love, a God who relents from sending calamity."

Jonah's refusal to go to Nineveh seems to reflect this warped thinking: "Lord, I'm not going to preach repentance to that good-for-nothing, wicked city of Nineveh, because if they repent, you will spare them. That's not fair! We're your chosen people; we're the believers. Outsiders don't have any right to your blessings of love and mercy. They're ours, remember? Besides, Assyria is our worst enemy. Spare them, and they'll come down hard on us."

Moses, Isaiah, and Jeremiah had tried to get out of proclaiming the Lord's message because they felt themselves unfit. But Jonah fled from the Lord and his prophetic office because his heart and mind were not in tune with the Lord's. He displayed a self-righteous exclusiveness. He looked upon God's blessings of love and forgiveness in the Messiah as something reserved exclusively for himself and his fellow Israelites. He also evidenced the presumptuous second-guessing of a misguided faith, refusing to do the will of God because he saw the results as being counteractive to what he believed was right and best.

There is a lesson here for us. What about the Jonah of bigotry and prejudice in us when it comes to sharing the gospel with others who "don't belong" or who "don't deserve it"? And what about refusing to follow the Lord due to questioning the results? That is one of Satan's favorite snares. Better to follow the Lord in everything, realizing full well that he knows what he is doing and that the consequences are under his control.

So Jonah "went down to Joppa," present-day Jaffa, some 30 miles northwest of Jerusalem and the only natural harbor on Israel's southern Mediterranean coast. It would have taken him two or three days to go the 60 miles from his hometown in Gath Hepher to Joppa, so his determination to run away from the Lord was no snap decision.

He refused to go the 600 miles northeast to Nineveh. Instead, he chose to take a Phoenician cargo ship that also carried passengers and headed west for Tarshish, over 2,000 miles away. Most scholars agree that Tarshish is another spelling for Tartessus, the ancient Phoenician colony on the southwestern coast of Spain. It is mentioned elsewhere in Scripture as carrying on maritime trade, particularly in silver, with Tyre of Phoenicia (see Isaiah 23:1; Jeremiah 10:9; Ezekiel 27:25).

To most people Tarshish represented the farthest known city of the ancient world. Located at the western end of the Mediterranean basin, Tarshish was the end of the line, so to speak, and that is exactly what Jonah was looking for. He wanted to "flee from the LORD" as far away as he could, to avoid serving the Lord as his spokesman in Nineveh.

The Hebrew says it better than the English: he wanted to "flee from *the presence* of the LORD." But the Lord is present everywhere.

> "Am I only a God nearby,"
>
> > declares the LORD,
>
> "and not a God far away?
> Can anyone hide in secret places
> so that I cannot see him?"
>
> > declares the LORD.
>
> "Do I not fill heaven and earth?"
>
> > declares the LORD.
> > (Jeremiah 23:23,24)

Jonah knew that. He confessed the Lord as "the God of heaven, who made the sea and the land" (1:9). He gratefully acknowledged in his prayer in chapter 2 that the Lord was with him in his watery grave. Jonah knew that, yet his fierce loyalty to his own Jewish nation and dread of the hated Assyrians had blinded him. Luther equates the presence of the Lord with the place where his Word, faith, and Spirit and the knowledge of God are. And this is also correct. Jonah was indeed fleeing from the spiritual presence of God's saving love and Word.

Or, more accurately, he was *trying* to flee, in the same way Cain tried to flee from the presence of the Lord (Genesis 4:16). Cain was fleeing in unbelief and despair from his only source of comfort and hope, the Lord. Yet the Lord would still be present with his grace and mercy, ever ready to receive Cain in forgiveness if he should repent. The same was true with Jonah. Trying to flee from God's gracious presence was spiritual suicide, but the Lord's loving compassion was not finished with him, as the rest of the narrative bears out.

The Lord corrects Jonah

⁴Then the LORD sent a great wind on the sea, and such a violent storm arose that the ship threatened to break up. ⁵All the sailors were afraid and each cried out to his own god. And they threw the cargo into the sea to lighten the ship.

But Jonah had gone below deck, where he lay down and fell into a deep sleep. ⁶The captain went to him and said, "How can you sleep? Get up and call on your god! Maybe he will take notice of us, and we will not perish."

Violent storms on the Mediterranean Sea are not uncommon, but this was a special storm. "The LORD sent [literally, 'hurled'] a great wind on the sea." It came from out of the clear blue sky with no forewarning. The Lord, who "makes winds his messengers" (Psalm 104:4), had a purpose in creating this violent storm, a purpose both for the sailors and for Jonah.

With their ship threatening to break open at the seams, the sailors were terrified, superstitiously believing the storm came from one of their angry gods. So they cried out to their Phoenician gods—gods such as Baal, the god of rain and thunder; Melgart, the god of the sea; Esmun, the god of ships and sailing. But they also tried to help their gods along by throwing cargo overboard, much as the sailors on Paul's ship did on his stormy voyage to Rome (Acts 27:18,19).

Jonah asleep

The sailors' efforts were to no avail. The captain wanted to try one last resort. Perhaps the passenger Jonah knew a god who had not yet been prayed to. "Get up and call on your god! Maybe he will take notice of us, and we will not perish." Let us not overlook the captain's opening words, "How can you sleep?" He had to go down into the hold belowdecks to wake up a sleeping Jonah.

Asleep during a raging, howling storm at sea, with the waves pounding and breaking over the battered ship! How could Jonah do that? Apparently, he had gone to sleep shortly after the ship began to sail, even before the storm. The hurried 60-mile trip from Gath Hepher to Joppa might have exhausted him. But so would the mental and spiritual agony he underwent in his determination to defy the Lord's call. So a tired and exhausted Jonah had gone belowdecks to sleep undisturbed. Did he also choose to sleep there hoping to remain unnoticed, hoping no one would remind him of his sinful disobedience? It's quite possible, and the fact that he could sleep during the storm seems to indicate he also had a sleeping conscience.

We cannot help thinking of a similar event in Jesus' life, when he also slept on a boat during a storm, on the Sea of Galilee (Matthew 8:23-27; Mark 4:35-41; Luke 8:22-25). It was not to hide in fear that Jesus slept, but because he had no fear of the violent storm that sent waves crashing over his boat. He slept the peaceful sleep of all who trust the love and faithfulness of the heavenly Father for full protection on land and sea or in the air. In addition, Jesus himself has power over the elements of nature, that they obey him, as his fearful disciples gratefully admitted.

What irony! A heathen ship's captain must call upon a prophet of God to wake up and pray when Jonah should

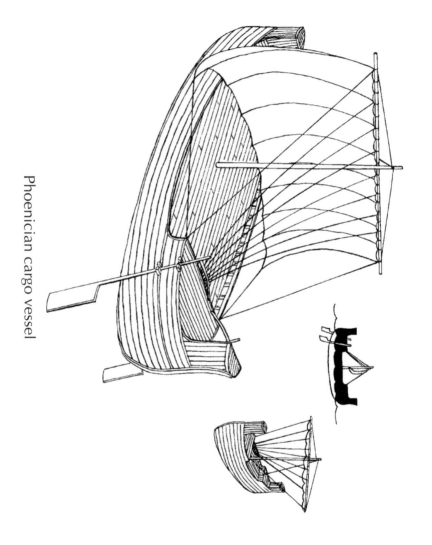

Phoenician cargo vessel

have been the first one to be alert to prayer. He was acting more like a heathen than the captain and his sailors! Whether Jonah then prayed, we are not told. At any rate, the situation was getting worse by the moment for him and the sailors. So another method had to be tried.

Casting lots

⁷Then the sailors said to each other, "Come, let us cast lots to find out who is responsible for this calamity." They cast lots and the lot fell on Jonah.

⁸So they asked him, "Tell us, who is responsible for making all this trouble for us? What do you do? Where do you come from? What is your country? From what people are you?"

⁹He answered, "I am a Hebrew and I worship the LORD, the God of heaven, who made the sea and the land."

Even the heathen, like these frightened sailors, have enough of God's moral law written in their hearts to recognize that sin calls for divine punishment. That is why the sailors cast lots. The lots were stones, pebbles, small balls, or pieces of wood of different colors, sizes, and shapes. When they were randomly cast into a circle drawn on the ground or into a container or were withdrawn from a container, a choice could be made by counting the similar lots for or against. Casting lots was a common practice among the heathen, used when looking for guidance and decision from some higher power. It was also practiced by the Israelites, more frequently in the Old Testament than in the New Testament.

In the Old Testament, the Lord commanded the Israelites to cast lots only in matters of great importance—choosing a scapegoat (Leviticus 16:8), distributing the Promised Land among the tribes of Israel (Numbers 26:52-56), and pointing out the guilty Achan (Joshua 7:14,15), for example. Sometimes to prevent confusion and quarrels, the Israelites on their own resorted to casting lots in minor matters, like choosing the order in which priests and Levites were to serve (1 Chronicles 24:7-18). The sole instance in the New Testament, the apostles using the lot to choose Matthias as Judas' successor, was not done by an express command of the Lord. He was, however, directly involved since the apostles prayerfully invoked his help before drawing lots (Acts 1:21-26).

The Lord did and, if he chooses, still can reveal his will through the casting of lots because he controls how they fall. "The lot is cast into the lap, but its every decision is from the LORD" (Proverbs 16:33). It would not be sinful for individual Christians or a congregation to use the lot to decide certain details in carrying out a project on which they are generally in agreement. In fact, such action might avoid a serious argument. "Casting the lot settles disputes and keeps strong opponents apart" (Proverbs 18:18). But since we have no express directive from the Lord to use lots, we cannot be sure the outcome reveals his will, even though the results may be good and honorable.

When "the lot fell on Jonah," however, it did reveal the Lord's will. Jonah was the guilty one responsible for the storm. Quickly the sailors plied Jonah with questions: "What do you do? Where do you come from? What is your country? From what people are you?" Jonah answered the last three questions at once: "I am a Hebrew," the usual term by which an Israelite was known to foreigners. His answer to their first question was a fitting confession of faith: "I worship the LORD, the God of heaven, who made the sea and the land."

Earlier, perhaps when he boarded the ship, Jonah had told the sailors he was fleeing from the Lord (verse 10). They no doubt looked upon Jonah's God then as just another local deity like one of their own, fickle and easily angered and therefore to be feared. Jonah's answer would correct that false notion. "My God is the true God, the Ruler of heaven and earth, of the whole universe. He is the Creator of the sea and the land and is therefore in control of the storm now threatening us."

Jonah may not have intended it this way, but his confession of faith would be used by the Lord to bring the heathen sailors to a saving knowledge of the true God.

Jonah overboard

¹⁰**This terrified them and they asked, "What have you done?"** **(They knew he was running away from the LORD, because he had already told them so.)**

¹¹**The sea was getting rougher and rougher. So they asked him, "What should we do to you to make the sea calm down for us?"**

¹²**"Pick me up and throw me into the sea," he replied, "and it will become calm. I know that it is my fault that this great storm has come upon you."**

Now knowing that they were dealing with the one true God, the sailors were terrified. "What have you done?" was a rhetorical question, implying, "Jonah, what's wrong with you? You dared to disobey the Lord! How could you invite all this trouble on us and yourself by thinking you could run away from the Lord who is everywhere?" Jonah's answer is not recorded. No doubt he had none, could give none, and just hung his head in shame.

At first, Jonah's answer to the sailors' next question comes as a surprise. "Pick me up and throw me into the sea, . . . and it will become calm." Was Jonah offering to commit suicide for the sake of the others? Was he practicing fatalism: "If my time is up, I'll die; if not, I won't"?

The rest of his answer gives us the explanation: "I know that it is my fault." Somehow, perhaps through the chiding of the sailors, the Lord had aroused Jonah's sleeping conscience and corrected him. Here is the first sign of Jonah's repentance, the frank admission of his guilt. He knew it was his fault. He also knew death was a fitting punishment for his sinful disobedience—but only if the Lord so willed.

He did not jump overboard, as some commentators suggest he should have done. He knew perfectly well his life was not his own. Not a suicidal death wish, not fatalism, but faith alone could move Jonah to say, "Throw me into the sea." He was no longer fleeing from the Lord. Now he was willing to commit himself fully, body and soul, to the Lord's gracious will and care. Jonah was willing to sacrifice himself for the sake of others.

The faith of the sailors

¹³**Instead, the men did their best to row back to land. But they could not, for the sea grew even wilder than before. ¹⁴Then they cried to the LORD, "O LORD, please do not let us die for taking this man's life. Do not hold us accountable for killing an innocent man, for you, O LORD, have done as you pleased." ¹⁵Then they took Jonah and threw him overboard, and the raging sea grew calm. ¹⁶At this the men greatly feared the LORD, and they offered a sacrifice to the LORD and made vows to him.**

In refusing to throw Jonah overboard as he had ordered, the sailors were showing greater compassion for human life than Jonah did when he refused to go and preach repentance to the Ninevites. But when their valiant efforts to row to safety were in vain and the storm intensified even more, the sailors realized very well that their only safety lay in the hands and will of their newly found God.

In contrast to their previous frantic prayer to their false gods, the sailors now prayed to the Lord with a remarkable degree of quiet confidence and faith, saying in effect, "We must throw Jonah overboard, Lord; you have made that clear. It's your will. You have always done as you pleased. But please don't hold us accountable, even though we deserve to die for causing an innocent man's death." Although they knew Jonah was guilty before God, they considered him innocent because they felt he had not harmed them. By nature most people know murder is wrong, yet the expediency of choosing the lesser of two evils is often used to justify murder, like that of abortion. But not so with the sailors. Their natural knowledge of the law was now sharpened by their newly gained faith in the Lord. To throw Jonah overboard was abhorrent and impossible unless the Lord absolved them of all guilt.

When they threw Jonah overboard, the violent storm stopped just as suddenly as it had begun. A miracle by the Lord? Indeed! It was a case of "stormy winds that do his bidding" (Psalm 148:8). The sailors recognized it: "At this the men greatly feared the LORD." This was not the fear of a slave cringing in terror before the lash of a cruel master, but the fear of reverence, the awe and profound respect of a grateful child before his loving father. The Hebrew phrase for *"feared* the LORD," then, means they worshiped him in grateful praise for his mercy in stilling the storm and saving their lives.

These formerly heathen Phoenician sailors were showing their newfound faith in the Lord, a faith that addressed him by his covenant name of saving love and mercy, "LORD," or Yahweh, a faith that recognized the sovereign power of the Lord and that submitted to his will. In that faith they now "offered a sacrifice" of thanksgiving, using whatever of value they still had on board the ship, and "made vows" of further loyalty and service to their Lord.

Among the miracles in the story of Jonah, the conversion of the sailors must rank high. Here was Jonah fleeing from the Lord because he did not want to share God's

PART TWO

The Lord's Deliverance of Jonah at Sea and Jonah's Prayer
(1:17–2:10)

The Lord delivers Jonah by a great fish

¹⁷But the LORD provided a great fish to swallow Jonah, and Jonah was inside the fish three days and three nights.

This verse is noteworthy on two counts, and both are unfortunate. First, it really should be verse 1 of chapter 2, as the Hebrew Bible has it, since it is more closely connected with the following verses than with the preceding. Second, it has become one of the best known verses in the Bible because of continual attack upon it by critics and scoffers. Scoffers see Jonah's survival in the belly of a great fish for three days and nights as an impossible story that borders on the ridiculous. As a consequence, they may very well laugh off the entire Bible as one big joke.

The critics, on the other hand, are not laughing, but their rationalistic approach to Scripture does not permit them to accept the miracle of Jonah in the great fish. Consequently, they try to eliminate all the supernatural in Scripture by reducing it to myth or allegory.

Accordingly, some critics regard the account of Jonah in the great fish as little more than a folk legend—something like the Greek legend of Andromeda and Perseus, where a beautiful maiden was offered as food for a sea monster and then rescued by a hero who slew the monster. Or there is the ancient legend of Orion, sailing to Corinth with his wealth. Facing robbery and murder by the sailors, he jumped overboard with his lyre and was saved by a dolphin lured by his music.

Other critics read Jonah as allegory. They see the fish as a symbol of King Nebuchadnezzar of Babylon, whom Jeremiah describes as a serpent that swallowed up Israel in exile and spewed her out again (Jeremiah 51:34).

Still others attempt to explain Jonah in the great fish as a bizarre natural happening. Jonah, we're told, found the carcass of a dead whale floating on the sea and took refuge in its gaping jaws. Or, he was picked up by a ship with a great fish as its figurehead.

Even some conservative Bible scholars have sought to explain the miracle as entirely natural and plausible. They point out that the sperm whale is big enough to swallow a man or even a horse. The largest member of the shark family is the whale shark, ranging up to 50 feet in length and 15 tons in weight; it could easily swallow a man. Then different accounts are alluded to, relating how people who have been swallowed by a large whale or shark survived when the creature was either forced to spew out its victim or was killed and quickly cut open.

There is a danger in seeking such explanations for this or any miracle of the Lord. It raises the temptation to make faith in a miracle depend upon some logical, natural explanation. But what if that explanation later proves false? Then faith is left to flounder. Faith needs no verifiable proof to rest upon. All it needs is the assurance "This is what the Lord says."

Our faith, grounded upon the Word of the Lord, will therefore accept the account of Jonah in the great fish at face value.

"The LORD provided a great fish," literally, God appointed, or designated, a fish in the waters of the Mediterranean to serve as his vehicle to rescue Jonah from drowning. Which particular fish God chose is not important. Nor is it important to understand exactly how Jonah could survive for three days and nights in the fish's belly. What a horrible experience for Jonah! Can you imagine being alive in the steaming hot darkness of the stomach, awash with pungent bile and reeking of half-digested food, where the only sounds to be heard are the thudding beats of your heart and the fish's?! Horrible, yes, but not really important. What is important to note is how God used his almighty power to work a miracle and carry out his purpose both for Jonah and for Nineveh. The significance of the three days and three nights will be discussed in Part Five of this commentary, in connection with "the sign of the prophet Jonah."

Incidentally, the Bible nowhere speaks of the great fish as a *whale.* That word was added to the vocabulary of the story by the unfortunate King James translation of Matthew 12:40, "For as Jonas was three days and three nights in the whale's belly . . ." The Greek word translated as "whale" simply means a sea monster, any large sea creature. So the NIV translates the Matthew passage correctly, "a huge fish." It is of interest to note that in the three passages in Jonah, the KJV correctly translates with "fish."

Jonah's prayer inside the fish

2 **From inside the fish Jonah prayed to the LORD his God. ²He said:**

> **"In my distress I called to the LORD,**
> **and he answered me.**
> **From the depths of the grave I called for help,**
> **and you listened to my cry.**
> **³ You hurled me into the deep,**
> **into the very heart of the seas,**
> **and the currents swirled about me;**

all your waves and breakers
    swept over me.
⁴ I said, 'I have been banished
    from your sight;
yet I will look again
    toward your holy temple.'
⁵ The engulfing waters threatened me,
    the deep surrounded me;
    seaweed was wrapped around my head.
⁶ To the roots of the mountains I sank down;
    the earth beneath barred me in forever.
But you brought my life up from the pit,
    O LORD my God.

⁷ "When my life was ebbing away,
    I remembered you, LORD,
and my prayer rose to you,
    to your holy temple.

⁸ "Those who cling to worthless idols
    forfeit the grace that could be theirs.
⁹ But I, with a song of thanksgiving,
    will sacrifice to you.
What I have vowed I will make good.
    Salvation comes from the LORD."

We have here one of the highlights of the book of Jonah, his ardent prayer from inside the great fish. Although we will consider Jonah's prayer by sections, we have chosen to quote it in its entirety to help the reader see its remarkable unity and development of thought.

This is a prayer Jonah spoke from the deepest distress of his soul as he tumbled into the depths of the sea. His prayer reveals his penitence, his faith, and his triumphant joy in the Lord's deliverance. It is a different Jonah speaking here in the belly of the fish than that who earlier had said, "No, Lord, I'm not going to do what you want!"

Note that Jonah's prayer is not a prayer for deliverance from the great fish. Rather, it is a hymn of praise and thanksgiving for having been delivered from certain death by drowning and from eternal death in hell. This observation will remove objections and difficulties some find in the prayer.

Jonah probably wrote the prayer down shortly after his deliverance from the fish. But he actually prayed this prayer while "inside the fish," expressing his thoughts in prayer fashion again and again, as he reflected upon his sinful action and the Lord's gracious deliverance. The prayer is a model in form:

1. It addresses the Lord of covenant grace (verse 2).
2. It brings a petition for help (verses 2,3).
3. It expresses hope and confidence in the Lord's answer (verses 4-7).
4. It concludes with thanksgiving and praise (verses 8,9).

It is interesting to note that Jonah based his prayer almost wholly on psalms written by David or others of David's time, which therefore were known by Jonah. Reference will be made to these individual psalms as we study Jonah's prayer. That Jonah could use these psalms with such ease indicates he was familiar with them from having used them regularly in his personal devotional life.

Jonah's experience reminds us of the blessing Christians have in committing Bible passages and hymn verses to memory. Sometimes the agony of sorrow and tribulation is so distressing that God's children cannot find words of their own to speak to God. In fact, their minds may almost seem to go blank. What a joy it is, then, to be able to retrieve from one's memory bank Bible passage after Bible passage, often from the psalms, as well as favorite verses from the hymnal. These treasured words not only comfort the heavy hearts and give strength to bear the burdens, they also enable Christians to tell God what is in their hearts.

We will now look more closely at the individual parts of Jonah's prayer.

Address and petition

²He said:

"In my distress I called to the Lord,
   and he answered me.
From the depths of the grave I called for help,
   and you listened to my cry.
³You hurled me into the deep,
   into the very heart of the seas,
   and the currents swirled about me;
all your waves and breakers swept over me.

Verse 2 gives a fine example of the structure of Hebrew poetry called parallelism. "In my distress" is parallel to and explained by "From the depths of the grave." So also, "I called to the Lord" parallels "I called for help." Finally, "and he answered me" parallels "and you listened to my cry."

Three times in his prayer Jonah speaks the name "Lord," the name of the covenant-God of grace and mercy. This is significant, because the name of the Lord is the basis for all true prayer. To pray in the name of the Lord is to pray in faith, believing that his redemptive death has opened the way to the heavenly Father and that he hears the prayers of sinners.

Jonah called to the Lord "from the depths of the grave," literally, from the belly of *sheol,* the Hebrew word for death, the grave, the abode of the dead. Jonah had felt as good as dead in his watery grave and cried out to the Lord, the only one who could help. And the Lord "listened" and "answered."

Jonah echoes the words of Psalm 30:2,3 (see also Psalm 18:6; 120:1):

> O LORD my God, I called to you for help
>   and you healed me.
> O LORD, you brought me up from the grave;
>   you spared me from going down into the pit.

When Jonah describes his distress by saying "you hurled me into the deep . . . ; all your waves and breakers swept over me," he is clearly recognizing his own guilt and the Lord's hand in taking just action to chastise him. The sailors threw Jonah overboard because the Lord moved them to. The Lord also caused the breaking waves of the sea to hurl Jonah "into the deep, into the very heart of the seas." The psalmist said,

> Deep calls to deep
>   in the roar of your waterfalls;
> all your waves and breakers
>   have swept over me. (Psalm 42:7)

A watery tomb in the depth of the sea seemed Jonah's certain and justly deserved fate, and there was absolutely nothing he could do about it, except to trust in his Lord.

Jonah's hope and confidence

> [4] "I said, 'I have been banished
>   from your sight;
> yet I will look again
>   toward your holy temple.'
> [5] The engulfing waters threatened me,
>   the deep surrounded me;
>   seaweed was wrapped around my head.
> [6] To the roots of the mountains I sank down;
>   the earth beneath barred me in forever.

But you brought my life up from the pit,
  O LORD my God.
⁷ "When my life was ebbing away,
  I remembered you, LORD,
and my prayer rose to you,
  to your holy temple.

Sometimes the Lord has to bring his loved ones to the lowest depths of despair before he can raise them to the heights of hope and joy. Such was the case with drowning Jonah.

As "the engulfing waters" surrounded him and the "seaweed was wrapped around" his head, tying him up like a bundle of firewood, Jonah felt himself sinking helplessly "to the roots of the mountains" of the sea. Jonah was speaking from a real-life experience. Oceanographers tell us there are high mountains rising from the seafloor as well as deep canyons plunging beneath the seafloor (see Psalm 18:15). When Jonah came to rest at the base of such a mountain, he saw the high cliffs above were barring his escape like the gates of a prison.

There he was, lying on the ocean floor, entangled in seaweed, slowly being covered by the swirling sand moved by the underwater currents, helpless, so very helpless! He clearly felt his life "ebbing away." But worse, he had to confess, "I have been banished from your sight." Jonah felt the seaweed of his terrible sins strangling him, dragging him away from the gracious presence of his Lord, where there is life and joy. What meaningful irony! Earlier he had tried to run away from the Lord's presence.

Helpless he was, but not hopeless. The Lord now aroused his faith from the depths of despair, stirred him to life so he could say with all confidence and hope, "Yet I will look again toward your holy temple." Jonah might have been thinking of Solomon's temple in Jerusalem, the focal point for the religious life of all Israelites, where the Lord was pleased to have his glory dwell (1 Kings 8:29,30). Perhaps Jonah was eagerly anticipating his return there for worship, and no doubt later on did so.

The word "temple," however, may have a less localized meaning here. It may refer to the temple of the Lord's presence, his dwelling place among people, wherever he shows his grace and mercy to those who worship him in faith. This is the Lord's gracious presence, always found in connection with his Word, by which he reveals himself to people. His presence means forgiveness of sins, life, and salvation in heaven. This is the meaning the psalmist has in mind when he says, "I will dwell in the house of the LORD forever" (Psalm 23:6). Jonah may have been thinking of Psalm 5:7 in his prayer:

> But I, by your great mercy,
>   will come into your house;
> in reverence will I bow down
>   toward your holy temple.

or Psalm 18:6:

> In my distress I called to the LORD;
>   I cried to my God for help.
> From his temple he heard my voice;
>   my cry came before him, into his ears.

Buoyed up by rising trust in his gracious Lord, Jonah remembered the Lord's goodness, the Lord's promise of forgiveness and life, and his prayer for deliverance rose to the Lord's "holy temple." The Lord heard his prayers and brought his "life up from the pit," saving Jonah from certain physical death in a watery grave, but just as certainly from spiritual death away from the Lord's presence. Jonah gratefully expresses the thought of Psalm 103:3,4:

> [He] forgives all your sins
>   and heals all your diseases,

[he] redeems your life from the pit
and crowns you with love and compassion.

Jonah's thanksgiving and praise

⁸ "Those who cling to worthless idols
forfeit the grace that could be theirs.
⁹ But I, with a song of thanksgiving,
will sacrifice to you.
What I have vowed I will make good.
Salvation comes from the LORD."

Jonah is making a general statement about the damning sin of idolatry in verse 8. He could have been thinking about the false gods the sailors prayed to when the sea storm arose. Their gods were "worthless idols," like those aptly described in Psalm 135:15-18 (see also Psalm 115:4-8):

The idols of the nations are silver and gold,
made by the hands of men.
They have mouths, but cannot speak,
eyes, but they cannot see;
they have ears, but cannot hear,
nor is there breath in their mouths.
Those who make them will be like them,
and so will all who trust in them.

Idols can be more than statues of false gods like Baal, Moloch, Ishtar, and Dagon, gods of the ancient Near East who were enshrined in silver and gold, made of wood and stone. An idol is often enshrined in the imagination of the mind. An idol is any thing, any being, any ideal or thought that takes the place of the true God and receives the love and trust that only God deserves.

Was Jonah perhaps thinking about himself? Hadn't he bowed down to an idol of his own making? Wasn't his defiant self-will a god that he followed rather than the will of the Lord? Surely he now knew how worthless it was; it did him no good whatsoever. In fact, he learned to his sorrow-ful regret that by worshiping his self-will, he forfeited the forgiving "grace that could be" his.

Yet, the Lord had brought his life up "from the pit" of destruction. Jonah could have expressed his deliverance in the words of Psalm 18:16:

> He reached down from on high and took hold of me;
> he drew me out of deep waters.

Jonah could only respond as every penitent sinner does, "with a song of thanksgiving," like Psalm 107:1:

> Give thanks to the LORD, for he is good;
> his love endures forever.

Certainly Jonah thanked the Lord for the mercy and love that had delivered him from a watery death and that he trusted would yet rescue him from the fish. And then, would we not expect Jonah to shout his loudest "Thank you, Lord" for delivering his soul from hell and damnation because of his sins, especially his self-will and disobedience?

Jonah also backed up his thanksgiving with "thanks-living," a sacrifice and a vow to his Lord, just as the sailors had done (1:16). We are not told what Jonah's sacrifice and vow was. A logical suggestion might be that he offered him-self to the service of the Lord, pledging never again to place his will in defiance of the Lord. And Jonah added "What I have vowed I will make good." It would appear that Jonah made good on his vow by his actions in chapter 3.

Like an organist playing a grand hallelujah-amen coda, like a powerful preacher in the pulpit bringing his stirring sermon to a rousing close, Jonah concludes his eloquent prayer with "Salvation comes from the LORD."

What could be a more fitting close than this central theme for the book of Jonah, yes, for all the books of the Bible? Salvation—deliverance from sin, death, and the devil—

comes only from the Lord, whose Greek name *Jesus* is related to the Hebrew word for "salvation." The sailors experienced the Lord's salvation. Jonah did as well. And soon the Ninevites would too.

There remained one last aspect of Jonah's salvation.

The Lord delivers Jonah from the great fish

¹⁰**And the LORD commanded the fish, and it vomited Jonah onto dry land.**

It must have been quite an experience for Jonah to be wrenched from the fish's belly by its regurgitation. But, we are confident, he didn't mind when he again saw daylight and breathed fresh air. Where the fish vomited him "onto dry land," we do not know for sure. Nearby Joppa, his initial starting place, seems as reasonable a location as any. For when the sailors tried to "row back to land" (1:13), they could not have been so far out from Joppa that such an attempt was inconceivable.

But let us not overlook the all-important phrase in Jonah's final deliverance: "The LORD commanded the fish." This is still the Savior's story. He is active in the lives of all his creatures—animals, plants, fish, as well as people. If only his rational creatures were as obedient as the rest of his creation!

With the miracle of the fish vomiting Jonah on dry land, Jonah's spiritual and physical rescue by the Lord was complete. Chapter 3 will begin a new chapter in Jonah's life, and in the lives of the Ninevites.

Before taking up that chapter, we must address an objection the critics raise against Jonah's prayer in chapter 2. They claim it is out of place and does not fit the context of the book. They see it as a later addition by an unknown editor, composing from the psalms what he thought Jonah might have said. The critics, therefore, suggest 2:1 was followed immediately by 2:10 in the original account.

We reply: If Jonah's prayer does not fit here, why did some later editor add it here as they claim? Furthermore, it does agree with the context very well. We must remember that it is a prayer of thanksgiving for deliverance from the sea and from his sin, not for deliverance from the fish. It also fits well by joining the two halves of the Jonah story into perfect symmetry.

PART THREE

The Lord's Second Call and Nineveh's Repentance

(3:1-10)

The Lord calls Jonah a second time

3 Then the word of the LORD came to Jonah a second time: ²"Go to the great city of Nineveh and proclaim to it the message I give you."

This chapter contains the climax of the story of Jonah, the conversion of the entire heathen city of Nineveh. In part because of such an unprecedented event, this chapter has also come under frequent attack by the critics and doubters. We will examine some of their arguments later.

But for now consider the amazing grace of God. The Lord gave Jonah a second chance and recommissioned him as his prophet to Nineveh. It is noteworthy that the Lord did not criticize Jonah for his earlier defiance and disobedience but passed over that with gracious silence. He saw the change in Jonah's heart and knew that Jonah had learned his lesson and was now ready to go to Nineveh.

Peter would later experience a similar reinstatement into his office as an apostle when the Lord told him, "Feed my lambs. . . . Feed my sheep" (John 21:15-17). When Peter called the Lord "the God of all grace" (1 Peter 5:10), he showed he fully understood how the Lord could recommission him by grace, pure undeserved grace. It was that way with Jonah too.

Jonah was to proclaim to Nineveh "the message I give you," literally, "the proclamation I am about to say to you." The first time the Lord told Jonah to "preach against [Nineveh], because its wickedness has come up before me" (1:2). The second time the Lord's directive to Jonah was less specific, implying the Lord would brief Jonah on the way regarding what to preach.

In retrospect we of course know what that message was: a call to Nineveh to repent or face God's judgment (3:4). The Lord's purpose in calling Jonah this second time was the same as before—to extend his saving mercy to heathen Nineveh, to move Israel to repentance by Nineveh's example, and to preserve Nineveh long enough to become a scourge of punishment upon Israel in case that nation would not repent.

Jonah preaches to Nineveh

³Jonah obeyed the word of the Lord and went to Nineveh. Now Nineveh was a very important city—a visit required three days. ⁴On the first day, Jonah started into the city. He proclaimed: "Forty more days and Nineveh will be overturned."

This time "Jonah obeyed the word of the Lord," apparently without hesitation or defiance, with no thoughts of fleeing from the Lord. What was he thinking as he made that long trip to Nineveh, a journey of over 600 miles requiring at least 25 days of travel? We would like to think he walked with a light heart of joy, buoyed up by thoughts of gratitude over the forgiving grace and renewed trust shown him by the Lord. Subsequent events show that Jonah still had problems with forgiving the Assyrians.

The great city of Nineveh

The NIV translation describes the city of Nineveh as "very important," suggesting an importance to God. This is one possible meaning—and a good one—for the Hebrew phrase "a city great to God," that is, great as far as God is concerned, great in his eyes, an object of his loving concern. God's words in Jonah 4:11 would seem to support such an interpretation: "Should I not be concerned about that great city?"

The Hebrew text reflects the other possible meaning: great as God is great, that is, the greatest, very great—an expression to denote the highest degree.

This meaning also fits well. Nineveh was a city great in power, culture, and size. It was the last capital city of Assyria, the largest gentile power at that time. Here were stationed the fierce troops and the swift cavalry of the king. The citizens of Nineveh felt secure behind its massive walls—100 feet high and broad enough for three chariots to be driven abreast on the roadway running along their top.

Nineveh may have had as many as a half-million inhabitants. Chapter 4 mentions there were "more than a hundred and twenty thousand people who cannot tell their right hand from their left" (verse 11). We understand this as referring to children who had not yet reached the age of discretion (Deuteronomy 1:39). Adding an older brother or sister and two parents to the family of each of the 120,000 gives a rough estimate of perhaps 500,000 inhabitants in Nineveh.

The city also contained heathen temples, magnificent palaces, parks, gardens and, later (650 B.C.), the famous library of Ashurbanipal, with more than 100,000 volumes. Ancient Nineveh was the New York or London of its day.

The size of Nineveh seems to be indicated by the expression "a visit required three days." Some have objected that this is an exaggeration, that the city never was so large. Well, that depends upon how one understands these words. The Hebrew text reads simply, "a city of a journey of three days," or, "of a three days' walk." There are basically three interpretations, and each has something to commend it.

1. The three days was the time required to walk the circumference of the city. Allowing a walking rate of 20 miles per day would give a circumference of approximately 60 miles for Nineveh. But the known circumference of the city was no more than 7 or 8 miles. Genesis 10:10-12 may explain this apparent contradiction. "The first centers of his [Nimrod's] kingdom were Babylon, Erech, Akkad and Calneh, in Shinar. From that land he went to Assyria, where he built Nineveh, Rehoboth Ir, Calah and Resen, which is between Nineveh and Calah; that is *the great city*" (our emphasis).

Apparently there was a "greater Nineveh" much like we speak of Greater Chicago or Greater Detroit, meaning the main city along with its outlying suburbs. Thus Greater Nineveh would have included in its administrative district the three other cities mentioned as suburbs, although Calah lay about 18 or 20 miles to the south. In all, Greater Nineveh would have covered an area roughly 20 miles by 6 miles, totaling almost 60 miles in circumference. Diodorus, a Greek historian of the first century B.C., also wrote that Nineveh had a circuit of 60 miles.

2. Another interpretation understands the three-day journey as the time required to walk through Nineveh; the phrase then refers to the city's diameter. Three days, however, would not be required to traverse Nineveh proper, with a diameter of no more than 2 miles, or Greater Nineveh, with an estimated diameter of 6 miles.

3. The three-day walk is interpreted by many to be the time required to travel the main streets and neighborhoods of Nineveh. It would then refer to the time it would take Jonah to complete his mission, going from section to section wherever he found people. This interpretation is suggested by the word "visit." We follow this as the strongest interpretation.

Jonah's message to Nineveh

So when "Jonah started into the city," he completed one-third of his three-day mission. Wherever he found people—in the doorways, in the shops, on the streets—he proclaimed, "Forty more days and Nineveh will be overturned."

Critics who challenge the historicity of Jonah claim the Ninevites would not have understood the Hebrew language Jonah spoke. Yet, both Hebrew and the Assyrian language belonged to the Semitic language family, so there was some basic similarity. In addition, one must remember Jonah may have spoken Aramaic, the language of commerce and diplomacy in the ancient Near East. Aramaic was spread by merchants everywhere. The Israelites were also acquainted with Aramaic (Isaiah 36:11). The question of what language Jonah used really is not important, since the text assures us that the Ninevites did hear and understand Jonah's preaching.

Was Jonah's message to the people of Nineveh just these eight words (only five in the Hebrew) and no more? We are not told, but in view of the results it is reasonable to assume that what we have here is only a summary of everything he said. But even this summary contains the truths of God's Word necessary for conversion, namely the law and the gospel. "Forty more days" was the gospel, stating the time of grace God was giving the Ninevites to repent of their sins and come to him for forgiveness. That the Ninevites subsequently came to faith (verse 5) and trusted in God's mercy for forgiveness (verse 9) shows the gospel had done its work.

"And Nineveh will be overturned" was the message of the law in Jonah's preaching. Implied was, "You have forty days to repent, but if you don't, you will be destroyed as God's punishment for your sins." That the law had its desired effect is shown by the fasting, sackcloth, and the dust (verses 5,6).

We can learn a dual lesson from Jonah's effective preaching. First, he was brief and to the point. He let the Word do the talking for him. He proclaimed God's law simply, directly, and with no holds barred. God does not trifle with sin but punishes it with his wrath and eternal judgment. Only when the severity of the law is realized will the sinner be led to truly grieve over sin and seek the Savior's forgiveness. Then Jonah proclaimed the gospel, again simply and directly. There is forgiveness with God because his Son died to pay for all sins. No further payment of any kind is demanded by God. No conditions are to be attached to the gospel.

Second, Jonah did not seek to draw attention to himself by his preaching. Note that once Jonah proclaimed his message, his name is not mentioned again in this chapter. At this point he was no longer important. Accordingly, the account does not say, "The Ninevites believed Jonah." Jonah did his job well; he let God have all the glory. What an admirable quality in a preacher—to impart to his listeners God's message so fully and clearly that he himself recedes into the background.

Is there any significance in the number 40 days? That's hard to say. The number 40 is often associated with testing and judgment. The rain fell for 40 days before God's judgment came in the flood (Genesis 7:4,12,17). Israel spied out Canaan for 40 days and wandered in the wilderness as a chastisement for her sins for 40 years (Numbers 14:34). Forty days was the time Jesus spent fasting in the wilderness before his temptations by the devil (Matthew 4:2; Mark 1:13; Luke 4:2). Likewise, Elijah traveled 40 days to Horeb in the wilderness of Sinai, where the Lord then instructed him (1 Kings 19:8). And Moses was on Mount Sinai for 40 days, begging God not to destroy Israel for her idolatry with the golden calf (Exodus 34:28).

Nineveh repents

⁵**The Ninevites believed God. They declared a fast, and all of them, from the greatest to the least, put on sackcloth.**

⁶**When the news reached the king of Nineveh, he rose from his throne, took off his royal robes, covered himself with sackcloth and sat down in the dust. ⁷Then he issued a proclamation in Nineveh:**

"By the decree of the king and his nobles:

Do not let any man or beast, herd or flock, taste anything; do not let them eat or drink. ⁸But let man and beast be covered with sackcloth. Let everyone call urgently on God. Let them give up their evil ways and their violence. ⁹Who knows? God may yet relent and with compassion turn from his fierce anger so that we will not perish."

Here is the greatest miracle in the book of Jonah and one of the greatest in all of Scripture. An entire heathen city is brought to repentance. Think of it—perhaps a half-million people, "from the greatest to the least," were led to confess their sins and turn in faith to the Lord for forgiveness! What a miracle of mercy!

The Lord gave Nineveh 40 days, but the city did not take that long to repent. Jonah had been preaching for only one day when "the Ninevites believed God." Jonah could not have reached the entire city in one day. Those who heard his message, therefore, must have carried word of it to others. Like a wildfire, the news spread. More and more kept coming, crowding around this strange prophet from Israel, eager to hear his even stranger message.

And they believed what they heard, because we're told they "believed God." As mentioned previously, Jonah's message no doubt was more than the eight words in verse 4. For the Ninevites to believe God, he must have told them about God—his person, his will, his forgiveness—as well as about their sin and its punishment. The Hebrew word for "believed" is the word from which "amen" is derived. In effect, the Ninevites said "Amen, it is true" to Jonah's message. They believed that the God that Jonah was preaching about was the one true God and that the message Jonah was proclaiming for this God was true and reliable.

Jonah as a sign to Nineveh

What aided the Ninevites in coming to this conviction of faith may very well have been the person of Jonah himself. In Luke 11:30 our Lord Jesus says that "Jonah was a sign to the Ninevites." A sign of what? In the parallel passage in Matthew 12:38-41, the Lord speaks of "the sign of the prophet Jonah" (verse 39) as Jonah's three-day survival in the belly of the great fish and connects it with his own resurrection from the dead. Somehow, perhaps by a report preceding his arrival in their city, the Ninevites had learned about Jonah's miraculous experience of being brought out of the fish alive. Jonah's "death and resurrection" was therefore a sign to the Ninevites that God had authorized his preaching. For them, he was living proof of the sure judgment and mercy of God, the heart of Jonah's message.

Entirely on their own, the Ninevites "declared a fast, and all of them, from the greatest to the least, put on sackcloth" as signs of their sorrow over their sin. It was a spontaneous act of their repentance. "When the news reached the king of Nineveh," he too recognized God's call to repentance and responded in a fitting way. He exchanged his royal robes for sackcloth and his royal throne for a seat in the dust to symbolize his utter humiliation before God.

But he did more. The king issued a decree to make the repentance a citywide observance. All were to fast and wear sackcloth, man and animal alike, the beasts of burden, the cattle, the flocks of sheep and goats. By not eating or drinking, the people were to keep their minds off themselves and their physical needs and reflect upon their spiritual poverty in sin. By wearing the dark sackcloth, usually made of coarse, prickly goat's hair, the people indicated their painful sorrow and mourning over their sins.

But why should the animals likewise observe repentance? They need no forgiveness. However, animals were considered a part of the person who owned them. Therefore, whatever they suffered was suffered by their owner. The lowing of the cattle and the bleating of the sheep, hungry and thirsty during their fast, was symbolic of their owner's cry for mercy and forgiveness. The Greek historian Herodotus (450 B.C.) describes how a Persian army mourned the loss of a cavalry leader by cutting off their horses' hair as well as their own. In the apocryphal book of Judith, reference is made to the Jews placing sackcloth on the altars and on their cattle for a day of prayer and penitence (4:10-12).

The king's decree also said, "Let them give up their evil ways and their violence," as a further sign of their repentance. Here is an admission not only of their sin but of the particular cruelty and violence that marked the Assyrians.

The king further decreed, "Let everyone call urgently on God," imploring their newly found God to accept their confession of sin and forgive them. "Who knows?" the king said. "God may yet relent and with compassion turn from his fierce anger so that we will not perish." These are important words for understanding the repentance of the Ninevites. "Who knows?" is not so much a question as it is an expression of hope. What the king implied was, "If God showed mercy by sending Jonah to warn our city, then there's hope he will accept our repentance and spare us and our city." These words of the king's decree express the Ninevites' trust in God's mercy. The king's decree is similar to the Lord's call to repentance issued by his prophet Joel to Israel:

> "Even now," declares the LORD,
> > "return to me with all your heart,
> > with fasting and weeping and mourning."
>
> Rend your heart
> > and not your garments.
> Return to the LORD your God,
> > for he is gracious and compassionate,
> slow to anger and abounding in love,
> > and he relents from sending calamity.
> Who knows? He may turn and have pity.
>
> > > (Joel 2:12-14)

We will want to look at Nineveh's repentance further. But first, critical scholars call several "problems" to our attention. The Jonah narrative cannot be historically true, they claim, because it speaks of "the king of Nineveh" when it should read "the king of Assyria." He was king over the entire nation, not just over the capital city. Our response is, the writer merely intended to refer to the king living in his capital, since Jonah's chief concern was with the city of Nineveh itself. The Old Testament often refers to kings this way. Israel's King Ahab was also called the "king of Samaria" (1 Kings 21:1). The "king in Damascus" was actually the king of Aram (2 Chronicles 24:23). Genesis 14:18 refers to "Melchizedek the king of Salem [Jerusalem]."

As a matter of record, the king of Nineveh/Assyria at Jonah's time was either the fourth king of Assyria, Adadnirari III (810–782 B.C.), or one of his successors, Shalmaneser IV (782–773 B.C.) or Ashurdan III (773–755 B.C.), depending on the exact time of Jonah's mission.

The critics also challenge the fact of Nineveh's repentance. It never happened, they say, since there is no historical record of it in any of the Assyrian inscriptions. Besides, they insist, it is absurd to expect an entire city of young and old to repent; it is psychologically impossible. By way of answer, we are compelled to ask the question, Must every historical reference in Scripture be corroborated by secular witnesses before we can accept it as factual? For centuries Isaiah 20:1 was the only known reference to the Assyrian king Sargon II. Yet today archaeology has shown him to be one of Assyria's most powerful rulers and the builder of a magnificent palace in Nineveh. There is likewise no secular record of the crossing of the Red Sea and the destruction of Pharaoh's army, no record of the fall of Jericho or of the slaying of Sennacherib's army outside the walls of Jerusalem. Yet they are factual.

The other objection, that a mass conversion is psychologically impossible, really means that such a conversion is humanly impossible. Of course it is! So is the conversion of an individual. Every conversion is a miracle by the hand of the Holy Spirit working through the Word. Psychologically impossible? So was the conversion of three thousand by Peter's sermon on Pentecost—many of whom just 50 days earlier had cried, "Crucify him, crucify him!" Psychologically impossible? "With man this is impossible, but with God all things are possible" (Matthew 19:26).

Was Nineveh's repentance sincere?

Some Bible scholars consider Jonah's message to be only a preaching of the law and no gospel. Consequently, they say the Ninevites never came to saving faith in the promised Messiah, and their repentance therefore was not true repentance. These commentators see the Ninevites' repentance as only terror of the threatened consequences of their sin and as an effort to avoid those consequences by any means, even by temporarily refraining from their sins and wickedness. But, the argument goes, the Ninevites never had true sorrow over their sins before God.

To answer this objection, we must remember that the word "repentance" is used in Scripture in both a narrow and a wide sense. Whenever it is coupled with "faith" or "believe," it has the narrower meaning: sorrow over sin. We see this in Acts 20:21, "They must turn to God in repentance and have faith in our Lord Jesus," and in Mark 1:15, "The kingdom of God is near. Repent and believe the good news!" Whenever "repentance" is used alone, however, it usually has the wider meaning: sorrow over sin *and* faith in the Savior for forgiveness.

We believe this is the type of repentance shown by the Ninevites. Consider the following.

Jesus said quite simply, "The men of Nineveh . . . repented at the preaching of Jonah" (Matthew 12:41). Since he makes no mention of faith or believing, it is fair to conclude that Jesus was using repentance in its wider sense: true sorrow over sin as well as faith in the promised Savior.

When the text says "The Ninevites believed God," it uses the same word for believing as is used in Genesis 15:6, "Abram believed the LORD, and he credited it to him as righteousness." Do we have evidence to say the Ninevites did not believe God with a saving faith similar to Abram's?

When they believed God, they believed that he was the true God and that his word was true regarding their sins and his mercy. Accordingly, they confessed their sins ("their evil ways and their violence"), they demonstrated sorrow over their sins (fasting, sackcloth, dust), they trusted in God's mercy for forgiveness ("God may yet relent and [have] compassion"), and they were willing to amend their sinful lives ("give up their evil ways and their violence"). Who are we to say the Ninevites did not display all the marks of true repentance?

The next verse brings us further proof of their sincere repentance.

The Lord's compassion

[10]When God saw what they did and how they turned from their evil ways, he had compassion and did not bring upon them the destruction he had threatened.

"When God saw what they did," he looked not only at the actions but also at the hearts of the Ninevites. As the one who searches the heart of man and examines his mind (1 Samuel 16:7), did God not recognize what he saw in their hearts? Did he not see true sorrow over their sins and faith in his forgiving mercy? He must have, because he recognized the fruits of their repentance, "how they turned from their evil ways," and "he had compassion" on them, forgiving their sins for the sake of the promised Messiah.

We are convinced the Ninevites showed sincere repentance and true faith and that God dealt with them accordingly when he "did not bring upon them the destruction he had threatened." Luther holds the same conviction: "Since the people of Nineveh believed the Word of God, of their own free will and with their faith as the leader and originator they did these works by which they gave external proof of their internal faith" (*Luther's Works,* American Edition, Volume 19, page 23).

Whether all the Ninevites of that generation continued in their new faith, we do not know. No doubt many grew careless and allowed their faith to be choked off like the plant in Jesus' parable of the sower (Matthew 13:20,21). At any rate, some 150 years later, in 612 B.C., Nineveh was destroyed. Were there any believers left then? We do not know; we can only hope so.

Does God ever repent?

What Jonah hoped would never happen did! "God repented of the evil, that he had said that he would do unto them; and he did it not." We have used this King James translation of the second half of verse 10 to bring up what some consider one of the most perplexing questions in the Bible: How can God repent?

The Hebrew word *repent* means (1) to have pity or compassion, (2) to feel sorry or grieve, (3) to be sorry for one's actions or repent, (4) to comfort or be comforted. The same verb root is found in the name Nahum (which means "comfort" or "compassion") and Nehemiah ("the Lord comforts"). It is used 38 times in the Bible, and in all but 8 of those times it refers to God's "repentance," not man's. The most common Hebrew word for man's repentance means to return or turn back.

The King James Version has helped to create the problem of God's "repentance" because it repeatedly translates the Hebrew with "repent" when referring to God. The NIV chooses different words, like "was grieved" (Genesis 6:6), "relent," or "had compassion" (Jonah 3:9,10), no doubt to avoid the problem of God's repentance.

It is a problem—as long as one thinks of God as repenting. But how can he repent in the sense of feeling sorry for his actions? He is free from sin; he never does anything wrong. Does the term mean God changes his mind? Not at all!

God is not a man, that he should lie,
    nor a son of man, that he should change his mind.
Does he speak and then not act?
    Does he promise and not fulfill?
          (Numbers 23:19; see also 1 Samuel 15:29)

If one chooses to say "God repents," the phrase must be considered an anthropomorphism. This is a way of speaking of God's actions in terms of man's actions, for the purpose of trying to better understand God. But because the phrase "God repents" is subject to easy misunderstanding, it is perhaps best to use a different translation as the NIV does.

What did the Lord do, then, when he *relented* and did not bring his threatened destruction upon the Ninevites? or when he relented and did not bring on his people the disaster he had threatened in the golden calf incident at Mount Sinai (Exodus 32)? In each case he had compassion on the people and withheld his judgment—at Nineveh because of their repentance and at Sinai because of Moses' intercession. In neither case did he change his mind. He did, however, change his course of action in keeping with his compassion and the conditional nature of his threats. He did not change his threatened judgment upon Nineveh. But when the city repented, his purpose was fulfilled and he withheld his punishment. The Lord explains himself well in Jeremiah 18:7-10:

> If at any time I announce that a nation or kingdom is to be uprooted, torn down and destroyed, and if that nation I warned repents of its evil, then I will relent and not inflict on it the disaster I had planned. And if at another time I announce that a nation or kingdom is to be built up and planted, and if it does evil in my sight and does not obey me, then I will reconsider the good I had intended to do for it.

PART FOUR

Jonah's Displeasure and the Lord's Rebuke
(4:1-11)

Jonah is displeased

4 **But Jonah was greatly displeased and became angry. ²He prayed to the LORD, "O LORD, is this not what I said when I was still at home? That is why I was so quick to flee to Tarshish. I knew that you are a gracious and compassionate God, slow to anger and abounding in love, a God who relents from sending calamity. ³Now, O LORD, take away my life, for it is better for me to die than to live."**

Chapter 3 ended on such a happy note, the miraculous conversion of Nineveh. We might wish the Jonah story would have ended there. But it doesn't. The book of Jonah began with God and Jonah, and now it will end with God and Jonah. Jonah had a problem, a serious problem, and with the same loving concern he showed toward heathen Nineveh, the Lord will now deal with his selfishly stubborn prophet Jonah. Nineveh repented. God was happy; Nineveh was happy. Jonah should have been happy too, for his preaching had helped bring great Nineveh to repentance and the Lord's salvation. But he "was greatly displeased and became angry." Why? A literal translation of verse 1 reads, "But it was evil to Jonah, a great evil, and his anger burned." "It" refers to God's sparing Nineveh. Jonah considered God's act of mercy a great evil. And now, like an angry judge, Jonah condemned God.

Jonah's displeasure was not an insignificant matter. He was thoroughly disgusted with the Lord's ways: "God, why did you show mercy to Nineveh? What have they done to deserve it? They are not God's chosen people like us Jews. They do not submit to circumcision and live by the other requirements of Jewish law. They repent at the last moment, and you bless them the same way you bless us. It's not fair, Lord, simply not fair!"

Jonah here was displaying one of the characteristics of a self-righteous spirit, namely selfish exclusiveness. The older brother in the story of the prodigal son had the same attitude. He angrily objected when his father received the wayward brother with open arms and then treated him like a king instead of like a prodigal (Luke 15:28-30). Remember Christ's parable of the laborers in the vineyard? The laborers who had been hired first charged the landowner with being unfair when he paid those hired at the eleventh hour the same wages as those who had worked all day (Matthew 20:1-16).

Selfishness and prejudice are very much alive today, even within the church. Have we ever felt reluctant to share the gospel with others because they're a different race? or because they live in the "wrong" neighborhood or speak a different language? Isn't it sad when some Christians resent it when the congregation receives a new member who formerly lived an unsavory life of sin? There should be joy, a thankful joy shared by the angels in heaven, over every sinner who repents (Luke 15:10).

Jealous exclusiveness resents sharing one's blessings with others or seeing them receive the same blessings. This was one reason Jonah was angry. He was Jewish and could not tolerate the gentile Ninevites receiving the same forgiveness, love, and mercy God had shown the Jews.

There was a second, perhaps more compelling, reason. Jonah did not want to be used by God to spare Nineveh so it could become a scourge that would later come down upon Israel. Jonah must have known some of the prophecies about Assyria someday destroying his nation of Israel. For example, the prophet Hosea had predicted that because of Israel's idolatry, the nation's idol (along with the nation itself) "will be carried to Assyria as tribute for the great king" (Hosea 10:6; see also Isaiah 7:17,20; Hosea 9:3). Jonah also must have heard reports of the horrible cruelties the Assyrians afflicted upon their captives. And he should go and preach to that cruel and wicked nation so that it might escape God's judgment and in turn bring God's judgment upon Israel!

In effect Jonah had said, "That's asking too much of me, Lord. I simply can't do it. I'd be a traitor to my own people. I'm not going to Nineveh!" But it happened! He did go to Nineveh, and—as Jonah had feared—God's mercy did spare the city. Jonah was thoroughly angry—at himself, at Nineveh, and especially at the Lord.

Yet, even in his confused state of mind, Jonah still knew enough to pray to the Lord. Sad to say, it was not a prayer of gratitude but of bitter resentment. Strangely enough, he admits his present anger and resentment was not the rash action of a moment but had been thought out long before, when he "was still at home" in Gath Hepher.

When he said, "I knew that you are a gracious and compassionate God," Jonah was speaking from personal knowledge. He had experienced God's grace and compassion. But he was also speaking from his knowledge of the Scriptures. Jonah seems to have quoted the prophet Joel almost verbatim:

> Return to the LORD your God,
>> for he is gracious and compassionate,
> slow to anger and abounding in love,
>> and he relents from sending calamity.
>
> (Joel 2:13)

Joel in return reflects the well-known words with which the Lord described himself when he gave Moses the second set of law tablets at Mount Sinai: "The LORD, the LORD, the compassionate and gracious God, slow to anger, abounding in love and faithfulness" (Exodus 34:6).

Jonah knew his Lord very well. He wanted God's love and compassion for himself and for his nation. But in Jonah's prejudiced way of thinking, the Lord made a big mistake when he showed love and compassion to Nineveh and relented of his threatened punishment. "Now, O LORD, take away my life." Jonah felt he would be better off dead than to see Nineveh spared. In chapter 2 he prayed and thanked the Lord for sparing his life. His prayer now does not thank the Lord for sparing Nineveh but asks the Lord to take his life.

When the prophet Elijah had crawled under a bush in the desert, he asked the Lord to let him die. He felt he had failed in his mission for the Lord (1 Kings 19). Jonah sought death because his mission had succeeded! In chapters 1 and 2, the Lord had corrected his wayward prophet by letting Jonah spend some time in the belly of a fish. Then "Jonah obeyed the word of the LORD and went to Nineveh" (3:3). Apparently, the devil did not allow Jonah's initial selfishness and prejudice to die out, but fanned their smoldering embers into full flame when the people of Nineveh repented and were spared. Unless corrected again, Jonah was in danger of dying spiritually. That his gracious and compassionate Lord would not allow.

The Lord's loving rebuke

⁴But the LORD replied, "Have you any right to be angry?"
⁵Jonah went out and sat down at a place east of the city. There he made himself a shelter, sat in its shade and waited to see what would happen to the city.

Here Jonah experienced firsthand that the Lord is "slow to anger." He did not take Jonah at his word. He did not kill him or let him die. Jonah was still God's child and prophet, wayward and misguided though he was, and he had to be corrected.

It is almost with a touch of humor that the Lord answered Jonah's prayer with the question, "Have you any right to be angry?" Here is the gentle voice of a loving and concerned father, "My son, stop and think about what you are saying. You say I'm unfair in showing grace and compassion to the Ninevites. Didn't I do the same to you when I delivered you from certain death? Now are you being fair? Is your anger at me justified?"

The Lord's penetrating question is addressed to us too, isn't it? We quite naturally seek to justify our emotions of anger as feelings we're entitled to. An unkind word or deed soon rouses anger with its self-justifying claim, "It's not fair; it's not right!" And we feel hurt. There is such a thing as righteous anger, but rightness is determined by God's will, not man's. Whenever feelings of anger begin to overtake us, we would do well to remember the Lord's question, "Have you any right to be angry?" Would the Lord want me to be angry?

Jonah gave no answer; he had no satisfactory reply. Yet, in a way he did answer the Lord's question. In disgust he "sat down at a place east of the city." Intertwining what few branches he could find, he made a crude hut for protection from the burning sun. There he "sat in its shade and waited to see what would happen to the city." Jonah simply could not accept Nineveh's being spared from destruction. The 40 days were not up yet, so he sat and waited, hoping and expecting God's judgment would still strike the city.

An object lesson for Jonah

⁶**Then the LORD God provided a vine and made it grow up over Jonah to give shade for his head to ease his discomfort, and Jonah was very happy about the vine. ⁷But at dawn the next day God provided a worm, which chewed the vine so that it withered. ⁸When the sun rose, God provided a scorching east wind, and the sun blazed on Jonah's head so that he grew faint. He wanted to die, and said, "It would be better for me to die than to live."**

⁹**But God said to Jonah, "Do you have a right to be angry about the vine?"**

"I do," he said. "I am angry enough to die."

As Luther says, now God began to play with Jonah as a mother plays with her distressed child to cheer him up.

God gave him a plaything as it were, a vine, as the focal point in his object lesson. Just what type of plant this vine was is hard to say. Some Bible commentators suggest it was some sort of gourd. Others say it was the castor oil plant, also called palma christi or palmcrist because its large leaves resemble the palm of a hand. That may well be. All we know is that it was some type of creeping plant with fairly large leaves. No Hebrew student reading Jonah in the original will ever forget its Hebrew name, *qiqayon*. But, like the fish, the identification of the vine is not important. God's use of it is.

God appointed the vine to grow miraculously to maturity in one day, "to give shade for [Jonah's] head to ease his discomfort." A gracious act of divine love and compassion and a step in the Lord's correction of Jonah.

Jonah had been uncomfortable, sitting there in his little hut. The hut branches overhead had soon given up their leaves to the sun, which now burned down mercilessly upon a sweating Jonah. He needed the shade of the Lord's vine. He also needed the comfort the vine afforded to be able to reflect upon his inner discomfort, the agonizing battle between his will and the Lord's.

"And Jonah was very happy about the vine." For once Jonah was happy. How quickly a small blessing from the hand of the Lord can ease our burdens and make us forget our troubles!

The Lord had not yet completed his object lesson for Jonah. The lesson plan was there, logically and orderly arranged. First he provided a vine; next he "provided a worm," some type of caterpillar or cutworm. The worm did what it was supposed to do. It "chewed the vine so that it withered" and died. Now where was Jonah's shade on the dawn of this new day? Since Jonah had refused to change his mind about the Lord's mercy, God resorted to sterner measures to teach him.

It should be noted that up until 4:6, God has been using his name of covenant grace and mercy, the name LORD, in his dealings with Jonah. At this point he proceeded to deal with Jonah as Jonah wanted him to deal with the Gentiles, using the name God, signifying his awesome power. He can create a vine, and he can destroy it. He is the Ruler of life and death. In verse 10 he will return to the use of his name LORD.

As the next step in his object lesson, "God provided a scorching east wind." When this hot, dusty, called a sirocco, begins to blow off the desert, it can raise the temperature by 20 degrees and drop the humidity in a matter of minutes. Its effect is exhausting.

Three times in this chapter it is stated, "God provided"—a vine, a worm, a scorching east wind—using the same verb as in 1:17, "the LORD provided the great fish." These are all natural means in themselves, but when they function at God's command, that is a supernatural act, a miracle.

Jonah's predicament was steadily growing worse. Sitting in his skeleton of a hut with no vine for protection, he felt the scorching east wind and the blazing sun. Before long "he grew faint" and "he wanted to die." As he waited for God's firestorm to destroy Nineveh, Jonah was risking sunstroke. But even more dangerous for Jonah was the spiritual battle being waged in his heart. His bitter disappointment expressed earlier in this chapter now became despair. But why was he despairing to the point of death?

Once again a gracious and compassionate God rebuked his wayward prophet with a penetrating question, "Do you have a right to be angry about the vine?"

Jonah's anger had been directed both against God and Nineveh. This time his anger is focused on the vine. How masterfully God had been teaching and leading Jonah! Now the loss of even a lowly vine affected him so deeply that he wanted to die.

Jonah's curt and snappy answer was, "I do. I am angry enough to die." This indicates the depth of his despair. Now the Lord had brought Jonah to the point where he could complete his object lesson.

¹⁰But the LORD said, "You have been concerned about this vine, though you did not tend it or make it grow. It sprang up overnight and died overnight. ¹¹But Nineveh has more than a hundred and twenty thousand people who cannot tell their right hand from their left, and many cattle as well. Should I not be concerned about that great city?"

Note the change in names. Once again it is the LORD, the merciful covenant-God, and not God, the almighty God, dealing with Jonah. He has made his point as God, the author of life and death. Now as the LORD of grace and mercy, he refused to surrender his prophet to despair and death. How could he? His love and compassion includes all, even a self-righteous Jonah. "As surely as I live, declares the Sovereign LORD, I take no pleasure in the death of the wicked, but rather that they turn from their ways and live" (Ezekiel 33:11).

The Lord's approach was this, "Now Jonah, let's look at this bitter anger of yours. You're angry out of concern for this lowly vine that has withered. Are you really concerned about it for its own sake? Like a gardener who has planted it, tenderly cultivated it, and watched it grow? Jonah, your concern for the vine is dictated by self-interest and not by love. You wanted the shade and comfort it afforded. Now that it can no longer provide that, you're filled with self-pity and self-righteous indignation.

"If even you feel so bad about the vine, how would you expect the gardener to feel, who carefully tended it and made it grow only to see it wither and die? Jonah, I'm God, the gardener who made that vine grow up overnight, remember? I have even more compassionate feelings toward Nineveh than you have toward the vine. All those people, all those cattle, Jonah—I made them too. I took care of them. I love them. Don't you think I should be concerned about that great city?"

What a masterful object lesson from the Master Teacher! Jonah's anger all along was centered in self-interest. Nine times in this chapter alone he had used the words *I, me,* or *my.* The Lord had to make him aware of this sinful self-pity as well as its companion in crime, prejudice.

There is an interesting parallel in the New Testament. At one time the apostle Peter had felt it was wrong to share the gospel with Gentiles or even to associate with them. In a vision God let Peter see a sheet coming down from heaven filled with food unclean for Jews. By this the Lord taught Peter the object lesson "that God does not show favoritism but accepts men from every nation who fear him and do what is right. You know the message God sent to the people of Israel, telling the good news of peace through Jesus Christ, who is Lord of all" (Acts 10:34-36). It is an interesting coincidence that Peter saw the sheet in Joppa, the same city from which Jonah had attempted to flee centuries earlier.

Some have wondered why the Lord mentioned the "many cattle" in Nineveh. His concern and compassion extends to all his creatures, even to the animal world. Sparrows do not fall to the ground without his permission (Matthew 10:29). He provides for the needs of animals, birds and other creatures (Psalm 136:25; 147:9; Matthew 6:26,28), and he preserves them (Psalm 36:6).

Animals have no souls and cannot sin. Therefore, there was no reason to destroy the animals in Nineveh. Nor was there reason to destroy the people in Nineveh. Although they had sinned greatly, they had repented, and the Lord had forgiven their sin.

Before leaving Jonah, we should mention another interpretation for the "hundred and twenty thousand people who cannot tell their right hand from their left." Some, including Luther, interpret these words to refer to all the Ninevites, who were children spiritually compared to the Jews. They did not yet know everything about God and his ways. Therefore, the Lord found it necessary to make allowances for them. We stand by our interpretation given earlier (see the commentary on page 66). These words describe the children in Nineveh who had not yet attained the age of discretion. Their number helps us to calculate how large the population of Nineveh may have been.

A lesson learned?

The purpose of the Lord's object lesson was to teach Jonah to love those whom God loves and to willingly extend to them the same grace and compassion Jonah had received. Did Jonah learn his lesson and repent? It seems so. To the Lord's question, "Should I not be concerned about that great city?" Jonah's answer was silence. One commentator has made the following observation:

> But his very silence on this point and the entire tenor of his book speak louder than words. Jonah would not have written so frank and self-humiliating a confession of his sin if he had not been sincerely repentant and had not hoped to preserve and save others from similar bigotry and grumbling. (Theodore Laetsch, *Minor Prophets,* page 243)

We would hope that a chastened but grateful Jonah returned to Israel to report on his experiences and to teach his own people the lesson he had learned: God's grace is universal, and Israel was to be instrumental in extending it to all. That lesson applies also to us. May we, who have come to know God's grace, eagerly share it with as many others as we can.

PART FIVE

The Message of the Book of Jonah

The book of Jonah solicits a great deal of response, not only because some see "problems" in the text but also because its message speaks to all people. We see this message as fourfold.

1. *Jonah foreshadowed the preaching of the gospel to everyone.*

The main message of Jonah has already been touched upon. God is "a gracious and compassionate God, slow to anger and abounding in love" (4:2). Notice that this passage does not state to whom God is gracious and compassionate, because there are no restrictions to his love. The universality of his love was promised in Eden and demonstrated on Calvary. Through the gift of his own Son, Jesus the Messiah, God has put his saving will into effect for all people. For he does not want "anyone to perish, but everyone to come to repentance" (2 Peter 3:9). The gospel of Jesus Christ, therefore, has no room for the selfish exclusiveness of a Jonah, the bigotry of national pride, the prejudice of race or social position. The apostle Paul makes this very clear: "There is neither Jew nor Greek, slave nor free, male nor female, for you are all one in Christ Jesus" (Galatians 3:28).

The book of Jonah is God's clear voice to all who have tasted his saving love, calling for them to share that love with others without the restraint of social customs or the prohibition of pride. Jonah reminds us to see all others as God sees them, as sinfully lost creatures who are the objects of his compassion no less than we are.

This first message of Jonah, then, is a strong encouragement for an active evangelism and mission program, one that does not pick and choose but faithfully seeks to witness to God's forgiving grace wherever and to whomever it can.

2. *Jonah was a picture of his nation, Israel.*

The second message of Jonah applies strictly to the people of ancient Israel, but knowing it will help us better understand the dual role God assigned this people.

In his wisdom God chose the Israelites to be his special people. In God's design Israel was to be the bearer of his messianic promise to provide a Savior for all people, Jew and Gentile alike.

To ensure that Israel would carry out this purpose, God isolated his people from the gentile world. This began already when he called Abraham, the father of the nation, to leave his home and people in Ur (Genesis 12:1-5). God further isolated the Jews by requiring of them the unique sign of circumcision as an unalterable condition of membership in his covenant nation (Genesis 17:1-14). He established a special relationship with them through his covenant at Mount Sinai (Exodus 19). For at that time he not only gave them the moral law to teach them his holy will but the ceremonial law and the civil law to strictly govern their worship and social life. These latter laws acted like a wall or barrier to separate Israel from the Gentiles, to keep his people religiously and racially pure (Leviticus 20:26). The ceremonial laws would cease with the coming of Christ, whom they foreshadowed (Ephesians 2:11-22; Colossians 2:16,17). The civil laws would no longer be in effect when Israel lost its status as a nation.

While God had chosen Israel and isolated her as his covenant nation, he did not intend at any time to restrict his saving grace to this one nation. All the messianic promises from Genesis 3:15 on were meant to include all people, Jew and Gentile alike. God repeatedly told the patriarchs, "All peoples on earth will be blessed through you and your offspring" (Genesis 28:14; also Genesis 12:3; 18:18; 22:18; 26:4).

Israel was to proclaim God's salvation to the gentile world by word and deed. By living separately from the Gentiles, Israel was to show them the saving wisdom and knowledge of God it enjoyed as God's people. "Observe them [the decrees and laws] carefully, for this will show your wisdom and understanding to the nations" (Deuteronomy 4:6). God intended that Israel was to shine among the nations with the light and glory of his salvation. In his prayer of thanksgiving when the ark of the covenant was brought to Jerusalem, King David reminded the Israelites,

> Give thanks to the Lord, call on his name;
> make known among the nations what he has done.
> Declare his glory among the nations,
> his marvelous deeds among all peoples.
> (1 Chronicles 16:8,24)

But the Israelites took too much pride in their status as God's chosen people. Like Jonah, they had blinded themselves to their responsibility to share God's saving grace with the Gentiles. They were content to keep it all for themselves in a self-righteous spirit of exclusiveness, a spirit shared in a perverted way by their later descendants, the Pharisees of Jesus' day.

At a time when Israel was coming into contact with the great powers of the east, Assyria and Babylon, God acted miraculously in Jonah's life to remind his nation to carry out her role of sharing his saving grace with the Gentiles. Jonah's initial disobedience pictured his nation's selfish reluctance to share their God with the Gentiles. So did Jonah's bitter disappointment after Nineveh repented.

When Israel failed to carry out this role among the Gentiles, it was to receive God's judgment through the instrument of the Gentiles. Thus the Lord's second purpose in sending Jonah to Nineveh was fulfilled when through his preaching Assyria was spared long enough to become God's scourge against Israel. Less than 60 years later God, would use the gentile Assyrians to punish Israel for her unbelief and for her refusal to bear his light before the Gentiles.

It is not difficult to make an application to ourselves and our times. God has given us the gospel as well as the resources to share it, while so many in the world are like the unbelieving Assyrians in Jonah's day. Must we not ask, "How long, O Lord, how long will you continue to bear with our lack of wholehearted passion for souls? O Lord, please give us the love and joy of the aged widow who said, 'I've had a bad day and don't sleep well at night unless I've told someone about Jesus or prayed for their souls.'"

3. Jonah was a type of Christ.

Here is the place to study Jesus' words recorded in Matthew 12:38-41:

> Then some of the Pharisees and teachers of the law said to him, "Teacher, we want to see a miraculous sign from you."
>
> He answered, "A wicked and adulterous generation asks for a miraculous sign! But none will be given it except the sign of the prophet Jonah. For as Jonah was three days and three nights in the belly of a huge fish, so the Son of Man will be three days and three nights in the heart of the earth. The men of Nineveh will stand up at the judgment with this generation and condemn it; for they repented at the preaching of Jonah, and now one greater than Jonah is here.

(See also Matthew 16:4; Luke 11:29-32.)

Christ had driven out demons—not only to prove that he is indeed God but also to show that he was preaching by the authority of God (Matthew 12:22-37). The Pharisees, however, rejected this proof and asked for a more compelling sign, some even more spectacular miracle. Jesus answered, "None will be given . . . except *the sign of the prophet Jonah.*"

This sign connects Jonah to Jesus by the three day and three night experience each had. In Jonah's case, the time he spent in the great fish may have been an actual total of three days and three nights, or 72 hours. In Jesus' case, we know the time he spent in the grave was less, perhaps a little over a day and a half. It actually was only the last part of Friday, all day Saturday, and a part of Sunday. This is no contradiction of Jesus' reference that he would be "three days and three nights in the heart of the earth." He was merely reflecting the Jewish idiom of counting a part of a day as a whole day in the listing of consecutive days.

The important feature in the sign of Jonah is what happened during and at the end of these three days and nights. Jonah was "buried" in the fish and "resurrected" three days later. Jesus was buried in the grave and resurrected three days later. Jonah, then, is a sign, or type, of Jesus' burial and resurrection, with the emphasis on his resurrection.

For the Ninevites, Jonah's miraculous deliverance from the fish after three days was God's stamp of approval on his mission and message. (See the commentary on page 71.) For the "wicked and adulterous generation" of Pharisees, Jesus' even more miraculous resurrection from the dead after three days would be God's authorization of his mission to die for sin and to establish the message of the gospel.

Jesus was "delivered over to death for our sins and was raised to life for our justification" (Romans 4:25). By raising

Jesus from the dead, God the Father testifies to one and all that he has fully accepted Jesus' death on the cross as payment for the sins of the world. By the same act he also declares that he stands behind the message of the cross, the gospel Jesus proclaimed in person and through his disciples.

It should be noted that the comparison between Jonah and Jesus eventually breaks down. Jonah's "death" in the belly of the great fish could not save Nineveh, but Jesus' death as the Son of God could and does save sinners.

The sign of the prophet Jonah, Jesus' resurrection, is a sign to be accepted or rejected. When the Jews rejected it, Jesus said the Ninevites would rise up and condemn them on judgment day. The Ninevites had less of a sign in Jonah's "resurrection" than the Jews did in Jesus'. Yet they heeded that sign and repented, while the Jews did not. Therefore, the Jews would be all the more guilty in the final judgment because they rejected the One who is greater than Jonah.

4. Jonah still is a type of Christ.

Jonah and the Ninevites are past history. But the sign of the prophet Jonah remains and will remain until the end of time.

It is a call to repentance. Christ's resurrection calls upon all people to acknowledge their sins, which made his death and resurrection necessary. It also invites them to accept his resurrection as divine proof that he did indeed die for their sins.

Christ's resurrection is a touchstone of the Christian faith. "If Christ has not been raised, your faith is futile; you are still in your sins" (1 Corinthians 15:17). Deny his resurrection and one denies his redeeming death on the cross. Accept it and his work of redemption is credited to the believer.

The importance of the sign of the prophet asks all who wear the name of Christ to take a long, hard look at themselves. Frank E. Gaebelein, in his excellent book *Four Minor Prophets,* says it well:

> We may study Jonah as a problem in historicity, we may debate the various ways of interpreting it, we may defend its miracles, we may scrutinize its text word by word; yet unless we take to heart its deep and wonderful meaning, we shall not only fail to be helped by it but we may even be harmed by our study. "O brethren," exclaimed G. Campbell Morgan when lecturing on this book years ago at Northfield, Massachusetts, "O brethren, how much of the attitude of Jonah is in us, without his honesty!" It is not only the unbelievers in the Ninevehs of today who need to repent; it is also we who are modern Jonahs. For no one begins to understand this profound and searching little book unless he discovers the Jonah in himself and then repentantly lays hold upon the boundless grace of God. (pages 126,127)

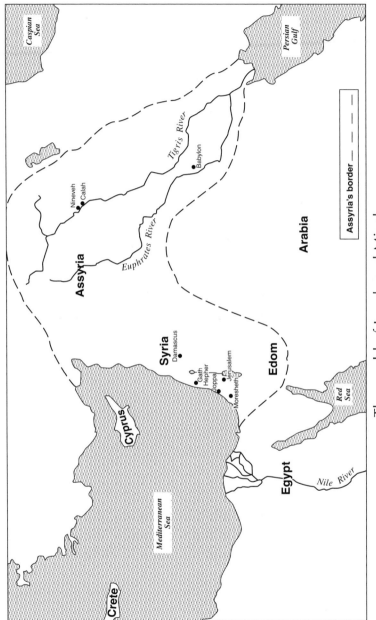

The world of Jonah and Micah

Assyria's border - - - -

97

INTRODUCTION TO MICAH

Micah was one of God's spokesmen during what has been called "the golden age of Israelite prophecy." His book consists of three prophetic addresses, each beginning with the command "Hear" (1:2) or "Listen" (3:1; 6:1). While differing in content and point of view, these messages are really not three separate prophecies delivered at different times. They are, rather, the sermons Micah preached, but in written form. In all three Micah rebukes the sins of his people, the Israelites, pronounces God's imminent judgment, and then promises his blessings through the coming Messiah.

Micah is quoted three times in the Scriptures. A century after Micah died, the elders of Judah quoted him (Jeremiah 26:17,18; Micah 3:12). In Matthew 2:5,6 the chief priests and scribes quoted Micah 5:2 in directing the wise men to Bethlehem. And our Lord Jesus quoted Micah 7:6 in sending out his twelve disciples (Matthew 10:35,36).

Author

We know very little about the personal life of Micah. All we know is what is stated in the opening verse. His name is a shortened form of Micaiah, meaning in Hebrew, "Who is like the LORD?"

His hometown was Moresheth, a small and insignificant village on the border between Judah and Philistia, about

25 miles southwest of Jerusalem. Because it lay only several miles from Gath, one of the chief cities of Philistia, it was also called Moresheth Gath (1:14). Today it is identified with the ruins of Tell-el-Judeideh.

Micah was therefore a small-town prophet who preached in the big city of Jerusalem. Yet he was not overawed by the size of this capital city or by its magistrates and priests. God had sent him to denounce the oppressive sins of Jerusalem and the rest of Israel. And he did so fearlessly, finding his strength in the Lord, as he confesses in 3:8: "But as for me, I am filled with power, with the Spirit of the LORD."

Date

Micah prophesied "during the reigns of Jotham, Ahaz and Hezekiah, kings of Judah" (1:1). This means Micah was active from about 739 to 693 B.C., before the fall of Samaria and well into the reign of Hezekiah. He was therefore a younger contemporary of the prophets Hosea and Isaiah. In fact, Micah and Isaiah have much in common. Both were prophets in the Southern Kingdom of Judah. At times their words are alike, almost identical, because they were dealing with the same subjects: the grievous sins of the people, and God's judgment and promise of restoration. They also wrote two of the most unmistakable messianic prophecies in the Old Testament. Isaiah predicted Christ's birth of a virgin (7:14), while Micah predicted his birth in Bethlehem (5:2).

Background and message

Like Isaiah, Micah belongs to a critical period in Israel's history, the latter half of the eighth century B.C. It was a time of political instability, social injustice, and moral degeneracy.

On the political scene, Judah had trouble with her sister kingdom to the north, Israel, as well as with Assyria, the world power occupying the lands of present-day Iraq and part of Iran. Israel joined forces with Aram, her neighbor to the north (later known as Syria), and invaded Judah. Together they slaughtered 120,000 of Judah's soldiers and carried off 200,000 captives (see 2 Chronicles chapter 28 for details). King Ahaz of Judah appealed to Assyria for protection. He got more than he bargained for. "Tiglath-Pileser king of Assyria came to him, but he gave him trouble instead of help" (2 Chronicles 28:20). In accepting foreign aid, Judah was forced to give up her independence and became a vassal of Assyria, annually sending off huge quantities of gold and silver as tribute. In 722 B.C. the Assyrian king Sargon II conquered Israel and its capital city, Samaria, and deported most of her inhabitants into the Assyrian captivity, from which they never returned. This event marks the end of Israel, the Northern Kingdom.

But mighty Assyria was not through with the Southern Kingdom of Judah. Twenty years after conquering Samaria, King Sennacherib of Assyria marched into Judah and besieged Jerusalem. Only the Lord's miraculous deliverance by his angel saved the city.

On the home scene, things were going from bad to worse. Under her 11th king, Uzziah, the father of Jotham, Judah had enjoyed a prosperity she had not seen since the days of King Solomon. But as happens so often, this new-found wealth brought with it social evils and spiritual poverty. It produced the extremes of a greedy wealthy class and a victimized poor class. Riches, luxury, and vice dwelt side by side with poverty, misery, and squalor. Conditions became so bad that there existed little mutual trust among family, neighbors, and friends.

These social evils were symptomatic of the spiritual poverty in Judah. Even the clergy joined the race for riches as priests and prophets served only for hire. Idolatry became widespread—among people God had chosen for his own! For many people, worship had become a mere formality, an outward observance of ritual and sacrifice considered sufficient to ensure God's favor, even if the worshiper's heart was far from him.

It was against such a background that the Lord sent Micah to speak to his people in Judah. Fully confident in the Lord's cause, he fearlessly denounced the corruption and heartlessness of the political and spiritual leaders of his day. Someone has described Micah as having Amos' zeal for justice and Hosea's heart of love. Micah was truly a prophet of the poor. But he was more! He was also a prophet of God's judgment and of God's salvation through the Messiah. He predicted the Assyrian captivity for Israel and the exile in Babylon and return for Judah, the bearer of the messianic promise. He referred to the profound spiritual peace the Messiah would bring when people "will beat their swords into plowshares and their spears into pruning hooks" (4:3). Micah expressed the faith of believing Israel and all believers when he wrote, "I wait for God my Savior . . . , who pardons sin and forgives the transgression" (7:7,18).

Outline

Theme: Israel's judgment and salvation

    I. God's threatened judgment and promise of deliverance (1:1–2:13)

   II. Israel's fallen condition and future restoration (3:1–5:15)

  III. The Lord's case against Israel and Israel's repentance (6:1–7:20)

PART ONE

God's Threatened Judgment and Promise of Deliverance
(1:1–2:13)

1 **The word of the LORD that came to Micah of Moresheth during the reigns of Jotham, Ahaz and Hezekiah, kings of Judah—the vision he saw concerning Samaria and Jerusalem.**

Like Obadiah, Jonah, and most of the other literary prophets, Micah begins his book by presenting his credentials. "The word of the LORD" came to him. It was important that the people whom Micah addressed would recognize that he was speaking with the authority of the Lord. By contrast, many of the prophets in Israel were false prophets who misled the people with their lies, speaking without the authorization of the Lord. Micah knew that some of the things he was sent to say were not going to be pleasant to hear. The country prophet from the little village of Moresheth, near Philistia, was going to proclaim God's threatened judgment on the leaders and the people of Jerusalem, as well as God's promise of deliverance. Micah needed the authority of the Lord's word.

Micah was active for about 35 years "during the reigns of Jotham, Ahaz and Hezekiah, kings of Judah." Jotham was basically a good king, but he impoverished his people by spending lavishly for luxuries and palaces. Ahaz not only tolerated idolatry but actively promoted it by introducing new false gods and rituals. Hezekiah has earned the name "good king Hezekiah" because he sincerely tried to reform his people, but moral and social conditions had become so bad that his reform was short-lived.

Because he prophesied in Judah, Micah does not specifically mention the kings of Israel, the Northern Kingdom. Yet God's prophetic vision to Micah included both kingdoms identified by their capital cities, Samaria and Jerusalem, because God still considered the people of both Israel and Judah to be his people.

Samaria had become the capital city of the Northern Kingdom about 875 B.C., when King Omri of Israel built it as his new capital city. He selected a site in the central hill country of Palestine, about 40 miles north of Jerusalem. He called his fortified city Samaria, a Hebrew word meaning "watch place," since it was located on a prominent rise 300 feet high with a commanding view in all directions. It remained Israel's capital for over two hundred years until it was destroyed by the Assyrians in 722 B.C. The village of Sebastiyeh occupies the site today.

Now Micah proceeds with his prophetic vision.

Judgment against Samaria and Jerusalem

> ² Hear, O peoples, all of you,
>   listen, O earth and all who are in it,
> that the Sovereign LORD may witness against you,
>   the Lord from his holy temple.
>
> ³ Look! The LORD is coming from his dwelling place;
>   he comes down and treads the high places of the earth.
> ⁴ The mountains melt beneath him
>   and the valleys split apart,
> like wax before the fire,
>   like water rushing down a slope.

Although Micah is going to pronounce God's judgment upon Israel and Judah, yet he calls upon all "peoples," the

103

"earth and all who are in it," to hear and listen, for this proclamation is meant for everyone. The Lord will use the two kingdoms as his "witness against" all nations who may be steeped in idolatry and wickedness like Israel and Judah. Indeed, all must acknowledge the Lord when he speaks from his "holy temple," his throne in heaven. He is "the Sovereign LORD," the one and only Ruler of the universe, with complete authority to condemn and punish sin. His standard for judging is his unchanging, holy will, written in the hearts of all men and repeated in unmistakable language at Mount Sinai. It applies to all people because God is no respecter of persons. But at the same time he is the Lord of covenant grace and mercy whose saving love reaches out to all mankind. Through Micah, he would repeat his promise of a Savior. This Savior would be born in Bethlehem (5:2) and would "break open the way" to heaven (2:13).

Let us not fail to note the strength of Micah's opening words. They set the stage for what follows.

With "Look!" Micah sounds a note of urgency—the Lord's coming is imminent, make no mistake about it. He steps out of "his dwelling place" in heaven "and treads the high places of the earth." Some have suggested that these are the high places where idol shrines were located. Most likely, however, the high places are simply a reference to the first places the Lord would touch in his figurative journey down from heaven.

To portray the destruction the Lord's coming in judgment would have, Micah uses the picture of destructive earthquakes and volcanoes: "The mountains melt," "the valleys split apart," lava flows like melted wax, "rushing down a slope." The Lord's judgment on sin is as sure and unavoidable as a river of molten lava flowing down a mountainside, sweeping everyone and everything in its path to certain death and destruction.

Because of their sins, all people must stand in fear of the holy God who hates sin and punishes it. Those who have seen his mighty hand destroy their homes and property and loved ones in mudslides and floods, tornadoes and hurricanes have special reason to stand in awe. They are acts of nature, yes; but it is a nature that God controls and uses to carry out his judgment. Let every crack of thunder, every bolt of lightning remind us of God's mighty power to punish sin and of our need to repent. At the same time, let's also remember that God used nature to help carry out his promise to provide a Savior. The Sovereign Lord of the universe is also the Lord of compassionate love and mercy.

Now Micah becomes more specific regarding the cause of God's judgment upon Israel and Judah.

> ⁵ **All this is because of Jacob's transgression,**
> **because of the sins of the house of Israel.**
> **What is Jacob's transgression?**
> **Is it not Samaria?**
> **What is Judah's high place?**
> **Is it not Jerusalem?**
> ⁶ **"Therefore I will make Samaria a heap of rubble,**
> **a place for planting vineyards.**
> **I will pour her stones into the valley**
> **and lay bare her foundations.**
> ⁷ **All her idols will be broken to pieces;**
> **all her temple gifts will be burned with fire;**
> **I will destroy all her images.**
> **Since she gathered her gifts from the wages of prostitutes,**
> **as the wages of prostitutes they will again be used."**

Micah here uses the term "Jacob" to refer to Samaria and the Northern Kingdom, and the term "Israel" to refer to Jerusalem and the Southern Kingdom. Both kingdoms were guilty before God because of their repeated transgressions and sins.

The prophet refers to their sinfulness with a series of rhetorical questions. Is not Samaria Jacob's transgression? Jeroboam, the first king of the Northern Kingdom, deliberately introduced idolatry into the worship of the true God to wean his people away from the temple and worship at Jerusalem. Later the capital city of Samaria became the seedbed of idolatry throughout the land. King Ahab with his wife Jezebel had introduced the licentious and degrading worship of the Phoenician god and goddess, Baal and Asherah. They even fed 450 of their priests at the royal table. Succeeding kings of Israel spread this abominable fertility cult throughout the land, until even the prophet Elijah thought he was the only faithful believer left. (See 2 Kings 17:7-17.)

Is not Jerusalem Judah's high place? Idolatry was formally introduced in the Southern Kingdom about 840 B.C. by King Ahaziah, grandson of King Ahab of Samaria. But it had been there earlier. Solomon had practiced idolatry along with his seven hundred wives (1 Kings 11:4-6). And other kings of Judah had tolerated the high places of Baal with their temple prostitutes.

The kings of Samaria and Judah were supposed to safeguard the true worship of the Lord. When they failed, they became responsible for the idolatry and wickedness of their people.

There is a lesson here for the leaders of the church today. The Lord has made them watchmen who are to warn their members of any spiritual danger (Ezekiel 3:17; 33:7). He holds them responsible to maintain the truth against all false teachings and practices. Yet, when falsehood rears its ugly head, does it not appear more often in the pulpit than in the pew? It has been said with some degree of validity, "As the seminaries go, so go the churches." The church must continue to pray for faithful pastors and teachers who are committed to the Word and whose only desire is to promote the truth.

When the Lord's hand of judgment strikes Samaria, her devastation would be complete. Stones from her destroyed walls and fortified towers would roll down into the surrounding valley 300 feet below, leaving her foundations bare. All that would remain of this once proud center of idolatry and wickedness would be "a heap of rubble, a place for planting vineyards." Shalmaneser V of Assyria began the destruction of Samaria in 725 B.C., and three years later his successor, Sargon II, completed it. Second Kings 18:9-12 gives the scriptural account. In his record Sargon would later boast,

> I besieged and took Samaria, led away as booty 27,290 inhabitants thereof, together with their chariotry. . . . The terror-inspired glamor of Ashur my lord overwhelmed them. At the very mention of my name their hearts pounded in fright, their arms lost their vigor.

The people of Samaria also lost their "idols" and "images." Whether these idols were carved out of wood or made from molten metal, the conquering Assyrians destroyed them. They also burned the "temple gifts," that is, the ornaments and other offerings brought to the shrines of the idols.

Micah's mention of "the wages of prostitutes" may refer to the cultic prostitution associated with the worship of Baal and Asherah. God clearly forbade temple prostitution by both men and women and specifically prohibited the use of their earnings in an act of worship (Deuteronomy 23:17,18). Or Micah may be referring to the spiritual prostitution Israel committed by breaking her vow of faithfulness to the Lord by worshiping idols. The prophet Hosea raises a similar charge in the ninth chapter of his book. In either case, everything Israel had used in connection with her vile idolatry the Assyrians would carry off to be used again "as the wages of prostitutes," to be placed in the temples of their idols and used for the sordid practices associated with their idolatry.

Weeping and mourning

> ⁸ Because of this I will weep and wail;
> I will go about barefoot and naked.
> I will howl like a jackal
> and moan like an owl.
> ⁹ For her wound is incurable;
> it has come to Judah.
> It has reached the very gate of my people,
> even to Jerusalem itself.

As Micah reflects upon the impending destruction of Samaria, he is reduced to a pitiful spectacle by his grief and sorrow. Weeping and wailing, he goes about "barefoot and naked," not nude, but stripped of ordinary clothes and wearing only rags, the garb of a mourner (2 Samuel 15:30) or of a captive (Isaiah 20:2-4). His groaning would sound like the mournful howl of "a jackal," like the wailing moan of "an owl," signifying that Israel's wound inflicted by the Lord was incurable. Assyria was coming to destroy her; there would be no reprieve.

Yet Micah's intense grief was also for his own people; he foresaw God's judgment on Samaria as a predecessor of his judgment on Judah. In fact, "it has come to Judah" and "reached the very gate of . . . Jerusalem itself."

God's judgment came upon Judah 20 years after the fall of Samaria. In 701 B.C., during the reign of Hezekiah, Sennacherib and the Assyrians invaded Judah. Sennacherib tells us in his own words,

As for Hezekiah of Judah, I besieged forty-six of his strong fortified cities. I drove out as booty 200,150 persons, young and old, male and female, horses, mules, donkeys, camels, cattle and flocks beyond counting. Himself I shut up as a prisoner in his royal city Jerusalem like a bird in a cage.

The scriptural account of the siege of Jerusalem is given in 2 Kings chapters 18 and 19, as well as in 2 Chronicles chapter 32 and Isaiah chapters 36 and 37. The city was spared when God sent his angel to kill 185,000 Assyrian troops in one night, forcing Sennacherib to retire to his homeland. But Micah did not have this foreknowledge. He only saw Judah being invaded by the same powerful and cruel Assyrians who would crush Samaria. Charles L. Feinberg comments, "Companions in sin are doomed to be companions in judgment. It is a solemn spiritual truth that we all do well to heed" *(The Minor Prophets,* page 155).

The last half dozen verses (10-15) of chapter 1 are absolutely unique in the Bible. Micah's lament over God's judgment on his people takes the form of a mournful dirge. The prophet names a number of cities in Judah that were going to feel the scourge of the invading Assyrians. He predicts their judgment in words that play upon the name of each city. We call this literary device paronomasia, or pun, a play on words. No English translation can really do justice to the Hebrew text since the play on words sometimes involves the meaning of the Hebrew names and sometimes the sound. The NIV footnotes reflect this feature. For example, it is as if Micah had said, "Watertown will thirst," or, "Madison has a mad son." We will attempt to indicate Micah's play on words by our parenthetical notations in the commentary.

¹⁰ **Tell it not in Gath;**
   weep not at all.
In Beth Ophrah
   roll in the dust.

No one should tell Gath ("Tell-town") about Judah's impending disaster so this enemy city in Philistia could not rejoice over Judah's misfortune. David urged the same course of action when King Saul and his son Jonathan were killed (2 Samuel 1:20). Indeed, Micah enjoins, "Weep not at all," so that the enemy will not learn of Judah's sorrow. Or, to follow the Greek Septuagint translation, "Weep not in Acco" ("Weep-town"), a maritime town between Tyre and Carmel. The inhabitants of Beth Ophrah ("Dust-town") are to roll in the dust, to symbolize their sorrow and shame over their coming disaster.

> **¹¹ Pass on in nakedness and shame,**
> **you who live in Shaphir.**
> **Those who live in Zaanan**
> **will not come out.**
> **Beth Ezel is in mourning;**
> **its protection is taken from you.**

The people in Shaphir ("Beautiful-town"), apparently a Philistine city, are not going to look very beautiful when they're taken away in shameful nakedness, according to the custom of conquering nations (Jeremiah 13:22,26). The inhabitants of Zaanan ("Exit-town"), south of Moresheth, will not leave their city when the enemy approaches—either because they're dead or because they're hiding in fear behind the walls. Meanwhile Beth Ezel ("Neighbor-town") would be in such deep mourning it would not open its gates to protect its neighbors.

> **¹² Those who live in Maroth writhe in pain,**
> **waiting for relief,**
> **because disaster has come from the LORD,**
> **even to the gate of Jerusalem.**

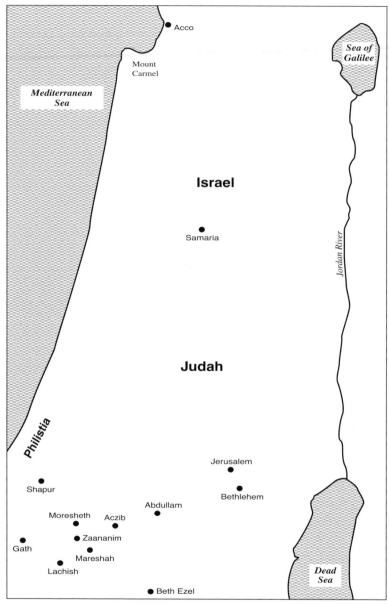

The homeland of Micah

In Maroth ("Bitter-town") people will wait in vain for relief when attacked. But all they will get is bitterness, since they deserve the judgment coming on them from the Lord. And this disaster would reach "even to the gate of Jerusalem" ("City of Peace"), undoubtedly a reference to Sennacherib's attack on Jerusalem in 701 B.C. If the Assyrians did not spare even the Lord's city of peace, how could Maroth expect relief?

> ¹³ **You who live in Lachish,**
> **harness the team to the chariot.**
> **You were the beginning of sin**
> **to the Daughter of Zion,**
> **for the transgressions of Israel**
> **were found in you.**

Lachish, about 30 miles southwest of Jerusalem, was the last Judean fortress-city on the trade route to Egypt. Lachish's strategic position made it a military and trading post. Horses and chariots were stationed here. Furthermore, Lachish may very well have been one of the "chariot cities" from which Solomon conducted his flourishing horse-trading business with other countries. These factors tend to support Micah's charge that Lachish was "the beginning of sin to the Daughter of Zion" (Judah). Interest in financial gain and contact with other nations could easily lead God's people into idolatry, as happened with Solomon (1 Kings 10:26–11:9). Later Israelites even practiced the idolatry of horses and chariots dedicated to the sun (2 Kings 23:11). In addition, the possession of horses and battle chariots could lead Israel to trust in them rather than the Lord. Idolatry and lack of trust in the Lord had become Israel's besetting sins (see Micah 5:10-14). Instead of trusting in horses and chariots for protection in time of war, the people in Lachish ("Chariot-town") are advised to use those horses and chariots to escape God's judgment—if that were possible.

> **¹⁴Therefore you will give parting gifts**
> **to Moresheth Gath.**
> **The town of Aczib will prove deceptive**
> **to the kings of Israel.**

How it must have grieved Micah to write these words! He sees his hometown, Moresheth ("Gift" or "Betrothal-town") being treated like a betrothed woman who is given farewell gifts by her father before she leaves his house. Moresheth would be lost to Judah as a bride is lost to her family. To the east of Moresheth, the Judean town of Aczib ("False-town") would live up to its name. As a stream that has run dry deceives the parched traveler who seeks its refreshing waters, so Aczib would prove deceptive. Under the Assyrian attack, it would fail to offer any help to the royal house of Israel who counted on its help.

> **¹⁵ I will bring a conqueror against you**
> **who live in Mareshah.**
> **He who is the glory of Israel**
> **will come to Adullam.**
> **¹⁶ Shave your heads in mourning**
> **for the children in whom you delight;**
> **make yourselves as bald as the vulture,**
> **for they will go from you into exile.**

Mareshah ("Conqueror-town"), located between Aczib and Gath, would likewise not escape the conquering Assyrians. In the end "the glory of Israel," her nobility, her riches, her military strength, all she was once proud of, would be compelled to flee to Adullam ("Refuge-town"), where David once fled into a cave to escape the sword of Saul (1 Samuel 22:1).

These solemn words of Micah point to an inglorious end for the cities of Judah, one that would bring shame and utter disgrace upon the chosen people of God. Therefore, the prophet exhorts his people to shave their heads "as bald as the vulture," whose head and neck are bare of feathers, as a sign of mourning and abject grief. Why? Because Judah will have lost the children of her delight, her people, "for they will go from you into exile."

Micah began this first chapter of his prophecy by pronouncing God's judgment upon both Israel and Judah. Israel's judgment climaxed in 722 B.C. when Samaria, her capital, fell into the hands of the Assyrians. God's judgment on Judah came in two stages. First, Sennacherib and the Assyrians invaded Judah and besieged Jerusalem in 701 B.C. This should have been a warning to the people to repent and return to the Lord. But they didn't. The second stage of God's judgment brought the climax. King Nebuchadnezzar and the Babylonian armies destroyed Jerusalem in 586 B.C. and deported the people into exile a thousand miles away from home.

It is strange that people never seem to learn the painful lesson of sin. God spells it out clearly in his Word: "Do not be deceived: God cannot be mocked. A man reaps what he sows" (Galatians 6:7). The most disastrous activity known to man is sin. Its consequences far outweigh that of all the nuclear warheads in the world detonating at once. "The wages of sin is death" (Romans 6:23)—physical, spiritual, and eternal death. Yet people play with sin as though it were a toy to be discarded at will. Sin's warning signs they so casually dismiss as applying only to others. Samaria of 722 B.C. and Jerusalem of 701 and 586 B.C. stand as mute reminders that

God's threatened judgment for sin is not to be dismissed lightly! Nor is his promise of deliverance from judgment through the Messiah. Ignoring the former inevitably leads to rejecting the latter, a tragic move that can lead only to hell.

In chapter 1 Micah boldly criticized the people's sins against the Lord. With an aching heart he announced the judgment of God awaiting them. In chapter 2 he goes on to rebuke with equal fervor the people's sins against their fellow Israelites. And again he predicts their just punishment. This time, though, he also points to One who alone could deliver them from God's certain and eternal judgment.

Man plans evil against man

2 **Woe to those who plan iniquity,**
    to those who plot evil on their beds!
At morning's light they carry it out
    because it is in their power to do it.
² They covet fields and seize them,
    and houses, and take them.
They defraud a man of his home,
    a fellowman of his inheritance.

Where there is no love for God, there is no love for people either. If a person's heart is empty of God, it is filled with greed and lust.

So it was among Micah's people. They not only committed idolatry against God, they planned evil against their fellow Israelites. The greed of the ruling and wealthy classes was restless. At night, instead of silently communing with God in gratitude for his blessings, they communed with greed, spending the entire night plotting other evil ways to get still more money and land.

"At morning's light," without a moment's delay, they eagerly set to work carrying out their plans. They were confident of success because they had the "power to do it." They controlled the dishonest judges and had power over the lower classes. It was no great task, then, to seize fields and houses by a simple show of might. They also used the corrupt courts to "defraud a man of his home, . . . of his inheritance" by a show of right. After all, doesn't might make right? King Ahab thought so when he used every means, even murder, to get Naboth's vineyard and satisfy his covetous heart (1 Kings 21).

When a man lost his farm, he lost his livelihood. When he lost his house, he lost his shelter. What did he have left in this world? He was either at the mercy of rich and merciless landlords, or he was forced into a life of crime to support himself and his family. When the rights of God are lightly treated, the rights of man fare no better. Witness Nazi Germany and communist Russia with their cruel disregard for human rights.

What shall we say about the United States? Rejecting God's will has produced a callous disregard for the sanctity of life. What other explanation is there for the murders, rapes, and other forms of violence that have infected society like a growing cancer? More and more people are assuming that human life is expendable. It's become like a tool to be used, abused, even discarded, as long as one gets what one wants. A pailful of dismembered fetuses in the abortion clinic or a mugged pensioner on the way to the store do not indicate a reverence for God's gift of life. May he speed the day when the United States truly lives up to its motto, "one nation under God"!

God plans judgment against evil men

³**Therefore, the LORD says:**

> **"I am planning disaster against this people,**
> **from which you cannot save yourselves.**

> You will no longer walk proudly,
>   for it will be a time of calamity.
> [4] In that day men will ridicule you;
>   they will taunt you with this mournful song:
> 'We are utterly ruined;
>   my people's possession is divided up.
> He takes it from me!
>   He assigns our fields to traitors.' "
> [5] Therefore you will have no one in the assembly of the LORD
>   to divide the land by lot.

When the ungodly plan iniquity against God's people, then God will answer them in kind. He will plan their "disaster" as a fitting punishment for their unrepented sin. This is in keeping with God's justice: "He will repay them for their sins and destroy them for their wickedness" (Psalm 94:23).

We have already referred to the disaster God planned "against this people": the Assyrian destruction of Samaria in 722 B.C. and the deportation of the people into exile; the Babylonian attack on Jerusalem in 701 B.C. and the destruction of the city, with the exile of the people in 586 B.C. From this judgment of God, the people of Israel could not save themselves, or as the Hebrew puts it, as slaves they could not remove their necks from under the yoke. In fact, as Jeremiah indicates, the captives taken at Judah were led into exile under a yoke (Jeremiah 27:12). Already at the time of Moses, God had predicted this would happen if the people turned away from him: "He [the Lord] will put an iron yoke on your neck until he has destroyed you" (Deuteronomy 28:48).

Arrogant and greedy landlords had preyed upon the people. All of this would be changed, Micah promised, when the "time of calamity" comes. Then they "will no longer walk proudly" but would have to endure the ridicule of their

117

countrymen. When the victimized and defrauded people saw their oppressors lose their wealth and property to the invading enemy, they would taunt and mock them. Pretending to be the ruined landlords and rulers, the people would mimic their laments of self-pity: "'We are utterly ruined' because our possessions and property are being divided up. The Lord 'assigns our fields to traitors.' How can he do that to us? We're his people! The Assyrians and Babylonians have turned their backs on the Lord. They're traitors!" How their sins of greed had blinded them to their own spiritual ignorance!

Micah replies for the Lord. In unjustly seizing the property of others, the ungodly leaders had forfeited their own. No one in Israel had the authority to divide up land for them. Now the enemy would do that. Another meaning for verse 5 suggests itself. The ungodly in Israel will have no further share in the inheritance of the Lord's people, that is, no share in eternal blessings. Indeed, "what good will it be for a man if he gains the whole world, yet forfeits his soul?" (Matthew 16:26).

Greed, evil plottings, oppression, and fraud are evidences of the hardened hearts of people who refuse to listen to the voice of God. Micah next rebuked his people for their shabby treatment of the Lord's prophets and his Word.

False prophets

> ⁶ "Do not prophesy," their prophets say.
> "Do not prophesy about these things;
> disgrace will not overtake us."
> ⁷ Should it be said, O house of Jacob:
> "Is the Spirit of the LORD angry?
> Does he do such things?"
>
> "Do not my words do good
> to him whose ways are upright?

False prophets, either corrupted by greed or controlled by the unjust rulers and wealthy landowners, rebuked Micah and the other true prophets: "Do not prophesy about these things—the wrath of God and his threatened punishment. Disgraceful things like that will not happen to us. We're his people. God can't mean what he says." What they really meant was, "We don't want to hear the truth about our sins. It's too painful."

In his answer to the false prophets, Micah addressed Israel as the "house of Jacob," to remind the Israelites how unlike their namesake they were acting. Jacob was a man of faith who clung to the Lord and his Word, especially in times of fearful uncertainty and grave crisis. Yet here were his descendants challenging the Lord's threatened judgment: "Is the Lord's anger so short that he cannot tolerate a few occasional lapses? Must he thunder immediate punishment for our sins? 'Does he do such things?' Doesn't he show mercy?"

Micah never heard the prophet Ezekiel, who preached in Judah over a century later. But if he had, he could have quoted Ezekiel in answering the challenge that the Lord is more eager to punish than to show mercy: "As surely as I live, declares the Sovereign LORD, I take no pleasure in the death of the wicked, but rather that they turn from their ways and live. Turn! Turn from your evil ways! Why will you die, O house of Israel?" (Ezekiel 33:11).

Speaking for the Lord, Micah explained how every word of the Lord is good for all who walk uprightly by faith. His law does good, even when it threatens punishment for sin. For then it drives the penitent back to the Lord for forgiveness. And, of course, his gospel is good, showing the unfailing love and mercy of the Lord who forgives sins through his promised Messiah.

God's justice

"How can God be a good God who loves people if he punishes them for their sins?" This challenge to God's justice is as ancient as humankind and as modern as today. Cain implied the question when God confronted him for the murder of his brother, Abel. He answered God, "My punishment is more than I can bear" (Genesis 4:13). Twenty-first–century sinful man declares, "If God really cared about us people, he would not allow wars, famines, hurricanes, or accidents to happen. And if that's not bad enough, then Christians say, 'He sends people to hell who don't believe in him!' He's not fair!"

What's missing in all these challenges of God's justice is an honest acknowledgement of the seriousness of sin and its deserved punishment. When sin is seen for what it is, disobedience of God's holy will and defiance of the One who demands perfection, then God will be seen as a just God who must punish sin. God is indeed just when he threatens, "The wages of sin is death" (Romans 6:23). Is he not equally just when he promises in his gospel, "But the gift of God is eternal life in Christ Jesus our Lord" (Romans 6:23)? His justice in the gospel is twofold: He punished mankind's sin with death, the sacrificial death of his own Son. And, he keeps his word of promise, "Believe in the Lord Jesus, and you will be saved" (Acts 16:31). Let all who want to challenge God's justice view their action in the light of both his law and his gospel.

Greedy merchants and heartless landlords

> [8] Lately my people have risen up
> like an enemy.
> You strip off the rich robe
> from those who pass by without a care,
> like men returning from battle.

⁹ **You drive the women of my people**
   from their pleasant homes.
You take away my blessing
   from their children forever.
¹⁰ **Get up, go away!**
   For this is not your resting place,
because it is defiled,
   it is ruined, beyond all remedy.
¹¹ **If a liar and deceiver comes and says,**
   'I will prophesy for you plenty of wine and beer,'
   he would be just the prophet for this people!

Like an invading army, the greedy and unscrupulous merchants, landowners, and court officials had risen as the enemy in Israel, an enemy of God and an enemy of the people. Ruthlessly, with no love for their fellowmen, they took people's "rich robe," the heavier outer garment that also served the poor as a covering at night. They confiscated "without a care" the garments of those who trusted them unsuspectingly or of the soldiers "returning from battle," too tired to argue and fight back. The merchants and landowners no doubt seized the garments as security for debts, a practice clearly limited by divine law (Exodus 22:26,27).

Again, with no regard for personal needs and feelings, the greedy landlords evicted defenseless widows, who lacked sufficient funds to secure their homes. How sad when they were forced to vacate the homes that had provided them with "pleasant" memories of their deceased husbands. And it was equally sad when in the process their fatherless children were deprived of their inheritances. The Lord had something to say about all this:

Woe to those who make unjust laws,
   to those who issue oppressive decrees,
to deprive the poor of their rights
   and withhold justice from the oppressed of
      my people,

> making widows their prey
> and robbing the fatherless. (Isaiah 10:1,2)

A nation that will prey on the helpless in its midst has forfeited all rights to continue to live in the land. It has "ruined" the land "beyond all remedy." Another translation might be: the defiled land "will destroy you with a painful calamity." Canaan was Israel's promised land of rest, where God intended his people to live in peace and safety, "each man under his own vine and fig tree" (1 Kings 4:25). But when they defiled the land with their detestable sins, God's will was specific: "If you defile the land, it will vomit you out as it vomited out the nations that were before you" (Leviticus 18:28).

No wonder the Lord announced through Micah: "Get up, go away" into exile in Assyria and Babylon!

Since the Israelites had rejected the message of God's true prophets, they were all the more ready to listen to the false prophets in their midst. These false prophets quickly learned that they could enjoy a comfortable living if they told the people only what they wanted to hear. So they prophesied messages pleasing to their listeners, promising "plenty of wine and beer," lives of ease and pleasure. Threats of punishment for sin never crossed their lips, because such preaching would get them no favors from the people. Micah calls such a prophet "a liar and deceiver," or somewhat more literally, "a deceiving windbag." That is the only kind of prophet the faithless people deserved, one whose prophecies had no more substance than a gas-filled balloon.

Time has not diminished the stature or the appeal of false prophets. Telling people only what they like to hear may produce a larger congregation or television audience—and maybe even a greater personal income—than telling people what God wants them to hear. People like to hear good tidings about themselves and the good they do. The social gospel makes for appealing preaching and comfortable listening. And when these prophets even disguise their falsehoods by quoting Scripture, their appeal becomes all the greater. Everything about them looks so legitimate. Overlooked amid all the religious airs, emotional rhetoric, and frequent showbiz hype of these false prophets is the sobering truth: False prophets "are not serving our Lord Christ, but their own appetites. By smooth talk and flattery they deceive the minds of naive people" (Romans 16:18). Thank God for true prophets, for pastors and teachers who speak the Word truthfully, who serve the Lord and his people and not themselves!

Deliverance promised

> ¹² "I will surely gather all of you, O Jacob;
> I will surely bring together the remnant of Israel.
> I will bring them together like sheep in a pen,
> like a flock in its pasture;
> the place will throng with people.
> ¹³ One who breaks open the way will go up before them;
> they will break through the gate and go out.
> Their king will pass through before them,
> the LORD at their head."

So far in chapter 2, Micah has been using the cutting edge of God's law in speaking to his people, denouncing their blatant sins with God's word of judgment. It must have come like a breath of fresh air to the penitent believers in Israel to hear Micah then speak the gospel, referring to God's gracious promise of deliverance through the Messiah.

His promise to gather a remnant of Jacob and Israel, his chosen people, at first suggests the return of the exiles from

Babylon in 536 B.C. And surely some of them were included. But since relatively few Israelites returned from exile, the gathered remnant here must have a broader meaning. It cannot, however, refer to the conversion of all Jews as some claim, for it speaks of only a remnant, not of the entire nation. We agree with Martin Luther's interpretation:

> After all, we certainly cannot take this passage to mean the restoration of the entire external people, as the words surely sound. This passage, then, will force and most certainly convince one that he must understand it to refer to a spiritual kingdom. For it was absolutely certain that the kingdom of Israel never was going to be brought back and restored. We do not read that it ever was restored, as the sacred histories show. Yet, although it was completely ruined and destroyed, the prophet is crying out about bringing back Jacob, a name by which he certainly means the entire populace. We are forced, then, to admit that the prophet is speaking about a spiritual gathering which takes place when the Gospel has spread throughout the world, to which scattered Israel is to be gathered together.
>
> (*Luther's Works,* American Edition, Volume 18, pages 227,228)

The remnant of which Micah speaks, then, refers to the spiritual Israel, all who are faithful to the promise God made with Abraham, the father of the Israelite nation. "If you belong to Christ, then you are Abraham's seed, and heirs according to the promise," Paul told the Galatian Christians (3:29). This latter-day Israel is none other than the New Testament church, made up of believers of all races and nations, all who have come to faith in the gospel of Jesus Christ.

The Savior's role is pictured as that of a shepherd, the Good Shepherd (see John 10). Through the gospel he gathers his sheep into the pen, that is, the church, the entire group of believers. And what an assembly! The church will throng with people, of all races and nations, so numerous they cannot be counted, all rejoicing over their deliverance (Revelation 7:9,10).

Micah describes Christ's deliverance as that of the shepherd breaking open the way before his sheep. The King James Version translates by calling the shepherd "the Breaker." This is an excellent picture of the work of the Messiah. By his life of perfect obedience and his innocent suffering and death, Jesus has broken down all barriers of Satan's stronghold that had held people captive. He has broken the power of sin, death, and damnation. The way to God and to heaven is open. Now his redeemed may pass "through the gate and go out" to serve him during this life and to follow him into eternal life. He, their Lord and King, will go before them, providing needed protection and offering guidance and comfort in his Word.

It would be a mistake not to mention the mission overtones in these last two verses of chapter 2. Jesus the Good Shepherd has said, 'I have other sheep that are not of this sheep pen. I must bring them also. They too will listen to my voice, and there shall be one flock and one shepherd" (John 10:16). It is the responsibility as well as the privilege of those of us who belong to the church to help the Lord gather his remnant, to add to the church his other sheep. The method? Speaking his Word so his sheep can recognize and follow his voice. All the Lord asks of us is to be the mouthpieces for his gospel. Is he asking too much?

PART TWO

Israel's Fallen Condition and Future Restoration
(3:1–5:15)

The leaders of Israel rebuked

With his attention-getting "Listen," Micah begins the second section in his book, chapters 3 to 5. In chapter 3 he will illustrate the sins he denounced in the previous chapter. His remarks are addressed against the leaders of the nation and are divided into three oracles: first, against the rulers (1-4); then against the false prophets (5-8); and finally against rulers, priests, and prophets (9-12).

Oppressive rulers

3 Then I said,

"Listen, you leaders of Jacob,
you rulers of the house of Israel.
Should you not know justice,
² you who hate good and love evil;
who tear the skin from my people
and the flesh from their bones;
³ who eat my people's flesh,
strip off their skin
and break their bones in pieces;
who chop them up like meat for the pan,
like flesh for the pot?"

"Those who plan iniquity" and "plot evil on their beds" (2:1) were not isolated cases among Micah's people. The entire structure of government and society in Jerusalem was infected with greed and violence. The "leaders of Jacob" and the "rulers of the house of Israel" included all the heads of authority in the church and in the state—priests, officials, judges, magistrates. The terms included even the heads of families and households. Every person in a position of authority has a responsibility to "know justice." For it is through the application of justice that each member of society is to enjoy God's blessings: a quiet and peaceful earthly life free from the threat of harm or loss and a full and rich spiritual life secure in the peace of God's forgiving grace.

In his Old Testament law, God gave the Israelites a clear and detailed basis for administering justice. It contained the moral law (the Ten Commandments), the civil law (government and social regulations), and the ceremonial law (church and worship regulations). Since Sinai these laws had been on written record. It was the responsibility of the priests to keep them fresh in the people's minds.

Instead of exercising justice, however, which requires hating evil and loving good, the corrupt and greedy rulers in Israel "hate good and love evil." Why? Because their hearts were evil. They were motivated by greed for personal gain and by lust for power.

It's not a pretty picture Micah painted of this cruel injustice against "my people," the God-fearing Israelites whom their countrymen hated for their moral uprightness. Micah depicted the rulers as acting like hungry cannibals in heartlessly oppressing the poor and innocent. There is no stronger simile in all of Scripture.

"Strip[ping] off their skin" and tearing "the flesh from their bones"—that's removing substance and shelter. Livelihood is destroyed when they "break their bones in pieces." Finally, when they "chop them up like meat for the pan," their helpless victims have lost everything, except their trust in the Lord. God had called Israel's leaders to be shepherds, caring for the special needs of his flock. At Micah's time, Israel's leaders were more like butchers, living off the flock.

Dishonesty, fraud, extortion, threats, foreclosures, exorbitant interest, corrupt courts, outright violence—the ungodly rulers in Israel practiced them all. They distorted justice so that they might fill their own pockets. What a contrast these leaders were to the self-sacrificing Good Shepherd in 2:12!

> ⁴ **Then they will cry out to the LORD,**
> **but he will not answer them.**
> **At that time he will hide his face from them**
> **because of the evil they have done.**

Micah's scathing denunciation would not go unnoticed. The day would soon come when in anguish the rulers would "cry out to the LORD" for deliverance from their impending judgment. But theirs would not be the cry of the penitent seeking forgiveness. "The evil they have done" was still with them. The Lord, therefore, would give them the answer of silence and hide the face of his mercy. They had shown no mercy toward their fellowmen; now they would receive none from the Lord. The apostle James states the divine principle, "Judgment without mercy will be shown to anyone who has not been merciful" (2:13).

Arrogant false prophets

> ⁵**This is what the LORD says:**
>
> > **"As for the prophets**
> > **who lead my people astray,**
> > **if one feeds them,**
> > **they proclaim 'peace';**

> if he does not,
>   they prepare to wage war against him.
> ⁶ Therefore night will come over you, without visions,
>   and darkness, without divination.
> The sun will set for the prophets,
>   and the day will go dark for them.
> ⁷ The seers will be ashamed
>   and the diviners disgraced.
> They will all cover their faces
>   because there is no answer from God."

Micah has already denounced false prophets in chapter 2 (verses 6,7,11). Now he gets to the very heart of their sin by pointing out their false motive and tragic deception. They "lead my people astray." Instead of leading God's people closer to him and helping them to remain faithful to his Word, the false prophets lead the people into sin and farther away from God. That's always the direction false prophets take with their wrong teachings, no matter how sincere they appear. Yet they claim to speak for the Lord! No wonder he calls these impostors wolves in sheep's clothing (Matthew 7:15).

Their motive soon becomes clear when the matter of their pay or reward is considered. God did allow his Old Testament prophets to accept reasonable compensation (1 Kings 14:3; 2 Kings 4:8). The false prophets of Micah's day were not looking for that. They wanted more, something to satisfy their expensive tastes. If they got it, they would gladly "proclaim 'peace'," a counterfeit peace. They would assure the people that God was not angry with them and therefore no calamity would befall them. But the very opposite was true. A century later Jeremiah found similar false prophets lulling the people of Jerusalem into spiritual complacency. "'Peace, peace,' they say, when there is no peace" (Jeremiah 6:14).

But whenever someone did not cater to the demands of the false prophets, "they prepare to wage war against him." They turned on him, like spoiled children who can't get their way. With false accusations and threats, they made his life miserable, even inciting others to persecute him, perhaps even to the point of death.

Because these prophets had misused their prophetic office, God's judgment would descend upon them like the darkness of night. That's the imagery Micah used to show how God would remove whatever prophetic abilities they may have had.

Four times, as if to emphasize this awful judgment, he uses similar expressions: "night will come," "darkness," "the sun will set," "the day will go dark." There would be no more visions of peace, no more enlightened knowledge, no more prophecies of any kind. All would be gone! The Lord Jesus described their loss this way: "Whoever does not have, even what he has will be taken from him" (Matthew 13:12).

On the day God steps in with judgment, all that the false prophets and diviners will have to show for their ungodly efforts will be shame and disgrace. "They will all cover their faces," most likely the lower half, as a sign of their shame, just as a leper had to do when he met a clean person (Leviticus 13:45). They will be disgraced "because there is no answer from God" to support their prophecies. The peace they promised never came. On the contrary, there was war and destruction (Micah 3:12). God's judgment came just as Micah had predicted. God's truth will always triumph over Satan's lies!

Micah, a true prophet

> ⁸ But as for me, I am filled with power,
>   with the Spirit of the LORD,
>   and with justice and might,

to declare to Jacob his transgression,
to Israel his sin.

How powerful and effective Micah was in contrast to false prophets! He was sent by the Lord; many of them were self-appointed. He was "filled with power, with the Spirit of the LORD"; they were filled with their own self-centered interests and duping powers. Their claims were hollow. The Spirit filled Micah "with justice," with a sense of what is right and just before God; their ideas of justice were self-serving. The Spirit gave him "might," the courage to fearlessly denounce the sins and transgressions of Israel, no matter what the consequences; the false prophets spoke only to satisfy the whims and fancies of the people.

This was not a boastful Micah speaking but a man made confident by the Spirit, ready to give God all glory. Luther displayed the same confidence as Micah, when before government and church he announced, "Here I stand; I cannot do otherwise." Every pastor, teacher, and missionary will want that same confidence the Spirit gives through prayer and meditation in the Word. Then they too will be able to preach the Word with power, admonish the erring, and rebuke the false teachers without regard for the opinions of people (2 Timothy 4:1-5).

Greedy leaders, priests, and prophets

⁹ **Hear this, you leaders of the house of Jacob,**
    you rulers of the house of Israel,
  who despise justice
    and distort all that is right;
¹⁰ **who build Zion with bloodshed,**
    and Jerusalem with wickedness.
¹¹ **Her leaders judge for a bribe,**
    her priests teach for a price,
    and her prophets tell fortunes for money.

**Yet they lean upon the LORD and say,
"Is not the LORD among us?
No disaster will come upon us."**

Here Micah sums up the charges he has leveled against
the rulers and prophets, and now adds the priests—all three
constituting the leadership of Israel. It is perhaps noteworthy that Micah does not mention Hezekiah who was king at
this time (Jeremiah 26:18). It is possible Micah chose not to
name him out of respect for his divinely appointed office as
king. Although Hezekiah was a God-fearing king who
began his career with a religious reformation, he seems to
have been powerless to curb the nation's greedy and ruth-
less leaders.

Micah had claimed to be filled with power and the Spirit
of the Lord. He now demonstrates this by meeting Israel's
corrupt rulers head-on. He minces no words when he
accuses them of deliberately despising justice and distorting
"all that is right." Perverting justice in the courts was a
favorite game of theirs. They practiced extortion, discrimina-
tion, cronyism, and legal "murders" upon the innocent and
unsuspecting. With this "bloodshed" of human misery and
woe, even actual murder, they built Jerusalem. The thought
here seems to be either they made a name for Jerusalem as
a wide-open city of "wickedness," or with their ill-gotten
gain they built luxurious homes for themselves in Jerusalem.
(See Jeremiah 22:13-17; Amos 3:15; 5:11.)

Micah focused on the chief sin that was common to each
of the three groups. In a word, it was greed. The judges and
magistrates could be bribed to deliver a favorable judgment.
This was something expressly forbidden in the Law of Moses
(Exodus 23:8). Priests had been appointed by God to
instruct the people in his Word without compensation. They
were to receive their sustenance from portions assigned

by the Lord (Deuteronomy 18:1-5). Yet here they were, teaching "for a price," thereby losing their impartiality. As Micah pointed out earlier, the false prophets could be persuaded to make favorable pronouncements "for money" while their services were supposed to be gratis.

It's a sad picture indeed that Micah paints of the leadership of Israel in his day! The love of money had corrupted the very people who were to demonstrate integrity by their example and to promote justice by their administration. What followed was the natural course of this sin: covetousness, deceitfulness, lust for power, oppression, and cruelty. Then they crowned their sin of greed with the sin of blasphemy. "They lean upon the LORD"; they rely upon him to back up their false claims and promises. "No disaster will come upon us" they boasted. "Is not the LORD among us?" This was like saying, "The Lord supports this kind of national life we have established in Israel, and his blessing rests upon us." God should honor and bless sin? God forbid! His judgment rests upon sin!

The destruction of Jerusalem foretold

The leaders had tried to build up Jerusalem by sin and corruption, but all they had succeeded in doing was bringing about its destruction.

> ¹² **Therefore because of you,**
> **Zion will be plowed like a field,**
> **Jerusalem will become a heap of rubble,**
> **the temple hill a mound overgrown with thickets.**

Complete destruction, utter devastation, a leveled city would be the result when Babylon's machines of war rolled over Jerusalem in 586 B.C. Read the historical account of Jerusalem's destruction in 2 Kings 25:8-21. Then turn to the book of Lamentations for a heartrending description of the horror and suffering of the people during and after the siege. Jeremiah's book of Lamentations begins with these sad words:

> How deserted lies the city,
>   once so full of people!
> How like a widow is she,
>   who once was great among the nations!
> She who was queen among the provinces
>   has now become a slave. (1:1)

While pointing to the wickedness of all her people as the cause for Jerusalem's destruction, Lamentations also calls attention to the role the false prophets played in her downfall:

> The visions of your prophets
>   were false and worthless;
> they did not expose your sin
>   to ward off your captivity.
> The oracles they gave you
>   were false and misleading. (2:14)

An interesting sidenote to Micah chapter 3 is that one hundred years later, Micah's statement in verse 12 was used to save the life of Jeremiah the prophet. When Jeremiah foretold the complete destruction of the Holy City because of the sins of the people, the prophets and priests and people wanted to kill him. But the elders of the land intervened. They quoted Micah 3:12 in arguing that Micah was not put to death for his God-inspired prediction, so neither should Jeremiah be executed. This account is given in Jeremiah 26:1-19.

Salvation for all on Mount Zion

A ruined and depopulated Jerusalem is not the final chapter in the history of God's dealings with his people. The God of just wrath and punishment is also the God of undeserved love and mercy. In Micah chapter 4, the Lord goes on to show his mercy by promising a restoration for all penitent people, Jew and Gentile alike, through the Messiah.

4 In the last days

the mountain of the LORD's temple will be established
as chief among the mountains;
it will be raised above the hills,
and peoples will stream to it.
²Many nations will come and say,

"Come, let us go up to the mountain of the LORD,
to the house of the God of Jacob.
He will teach us his ways,
so that we may walk in his paths."
The law will go out from Zion,
the word of the LORD from Jerusalem.

These words are almost identical to Isaiah's words (2:2-4). Bible scholars debate who wrote them first, Isaiah or Micah, and who borrowed from whom. Luther believed Micah was the older of the two and therefore wrote first. Others agree but for another reason, namely, that the verses fit better into the context of Micah's prophecy. It's impossible to know who wrote first, and really there's no great need to know. It is sufficient to know that both Micah and Isaiah wrote by inspiration of God.

The phrase "in the last days," when used by the prophets, refers to the time of the Messiah, marking the end of the Jewish age and introducing the New Testament era. (See, for example, Hosea 3:5; Acts 2:17.) Then "the mountain of the LORD's temple" will be established. The temple on Mount Zion, destroyed along with Jerusalem by the Babylonians, would one day be rebuilt by the returning exiles (516 B.C.).

But that is not the temple Micah was referring to, nor was he predicting the external restoration of the nation of Israel, as many today hold. He was predicting the establishment of the spiritual Mount Zion, the New Testament church founded upon Jesus Christ (Ephesians 2:19-22).

Micah notes three characteristics of the New Testament church. (1) It will be "chief among the mountains," superior to all other kingdoms, secular and religious. Already in the Old Testament, God's saving kingdom had a superior glory. But the New Testament church would exceed the glory of the old covenant by abolishing its ceremonial regulations in the person of Jesus Christ (Colossians 2:9-17). (2) "It will be raised above the hills," that is, it would be of a different nature than other kingdoms that are here today and gone tomorrow. Christ's kingdom will be permanent, established forever (Psalm 45:6; Daniel 2:44). (3) "Peoples will stream to it." The church of Jesus Christ will be universal, for all people. Time, race, sex, age, and geographical boundaries will have no bearing on the extent of Messiah's rule in the hearts of people (Romans 10:12,13; Colossians 3:11).

The new Mount Zion will be universal through its proclamation of the gospel. Therefore, people of "many nations" will encourage one another to "go up to the mountain of the LORD," to come under the saving influence of the gospel. Here is a reference to the domino effect of mission work. As the unchurched are won for Christ through the gospel, they in turn invite other unchurched to come to Christ for salvation. The gospel produces its own missionaries.

All who become members of the Messiah's kingdom will partake of the blessings of his Word. "He will teach us his ways," all we need to know about God and his will, about ourselves and our world, everything necessary for salvation and a God-pleasing life. In fact, his Word and Spirit give us the strength to "walk in his paths" (see Psalm 23:3; 51:10). In gratitude for their salvation the members of the church then are eager to see the Word "go out from Zion" to share its blessings with others.

> ³ He will judge between many peoples
>   and will settle disputes for strong nations far and wide.
> They will beat their swords into plowshares
>   and their spears into pruning hooks.
> Nation will not take up sword against nation,
>   nor will they train for war anymore.
> ⁴ Every man will sit under his own vine
>   and under his own fig tree,
> and no one will make them afraid,
>   for the LORD Almighty has spoken.
> ⁵ All the nations may walk
>   in the name of their gods;
> we will walk in the name of the LORD
>   our God for ever and ever.

Verse 3 of this chapter has been erroneously interpreted as promising worldwide political and social peace as a result of the preaching of the gospel. It's a pleasing thought, but quite contrary to what Scripture says. The gospel may, in fact, cause divisions and discord, even in close-knit families, because some accept it while others do not (Matthew 10:34-36). "He will judge between many peoples and will settle disputes for strong nations" through his Word, the same gospel that goes out from Mount Zion, the church of believers. He will judge between those who in faith accept his Word and those who do not; he will rebuke (another meaning for "settle disputes") those who reject it.

The result for the members of Christ's church will be peace. Micah describes this peace in several ways. When nations no longer go to war but "beat their swords into plowshares," they turn their war energies into domestic pursuits. In a similar way, believers will display an attitude of peace toward the people and nations in the world. Christ's kingdom is a spiritual kingdom of peace, which does not exist by the sword (John 18:36). Consequently, believers will do nothing to cause the world around them to take up the sword but will try to live at peace with one another (Romans 12:18). There is good reason for the church not to enter the social and political arena to fight for its concerns. The results will be anything but peaceful.

Both the vine and the fig tree form natural arbors where an ancient Israelite might sit in quiet solitude. Sitting under one's own vine and fig tree refers to the inner peace and solitude the Christian possesses because he knows that the Savior's life and death have made peace between him and God. That's why nothing and no one—not even sin, death, or Satan himself—"will make them afraid" (see Isaiah 41:10; Psalm 23:4).

The peace found alone in the Christian church is no mere wishful thinking, like the unattainable dream of the United Nations for world peace; often their deliberations are anything but peaceful. Nor is the peace Christ brings a fragile peace easily broken by a change in moods, like that which exists in some homes. It is a peace "the LORD Almighty has spoken." His word of promise declares it as fact: "Since we have been justified through faith, we have peace with God through our Lord Jesus Christ" (Romans 5:1).

When "all the nations . . . walk in the name of their gods," then their purposes and goals, their political ideals and their lifestyles reflect the character of those false gods. And that character is never peace but invariably strife and discord. It cannot be otherwise. "There is no peace," says God, "for the wicked" (Isaiah 57:21). The members of Christ's kingdom "will walk in the name of the LORD our God for ever and ever." Walking by faith in the gospel, the believers have an everlasting peace because they have the sure promise of eternal life through Jesus Christ.

The Lord's plan for the restoration of Jerusalem

⁶"In that day," declares the LORD,

"I will gather the lame;
I will assemble the exiles
and those I have brought to grief.
⁷ I will make the lame a remnant,
those driven away a strong nation.
The LORD will rule over them in Mount Zion
from that day and forever.
⁸ As for you, O watchtower of the flock,
O stronghold of the Daughter of Zion,
the former dominion will be restored to you;
kingship will come to the Daughter of Jerusalem."

In these verses the prophet again takes up the thought that the Lord will gather the remnant of Israel, which he had mentioned in 2:12. The remnant are said to be "lame" like Jacob was after he wrestled with God, as a sign of his own weakness (Genesis 32:31). In the same way, the members of the church also show weakness and need God's discipline. The Lord made his people lame by bringing them to grief and driving them into exile. But as their Lord of love and mercy, he did not allow them to languish helplessly. He brought the remnant back and made it "a strong nation."

As stated earlier, the returning remnant does not refer primarily to those Jews who returned from exile. To be sure, the faithful among them were included. The expression, however, includes all whom the Lord in his grace calls to faith, who are thus gathered into his family. The remnant, then, are the few Jesus spoke of when he said, "Many are invited, but few are chosen" (Matthew 22:14).

Accordingly, their strength is not in their numbers, but in the Lord who will "rule over them in Mount Zion from that day and forever." By the death of his Son, God has made his New Testament church eternal and impregnable against all foes, even against the gates of hell (Matthew 16:18).

The Lord's gracious rule over his church is described as a "watchtower of the flock." This is an allusion to the ancient practice of building sentry towers to watch over vineyards and over sheep or cattle out in the field (2 Chronicles 26:10). The Messiah, the Good Shepherd (Micah 2:12), watches carefully over his remnant from his tower in Mount Zion, the church. Here "the former," or earlier, kingdom promised to the patriarchs and to David (2 Samuel 7:16) will be restored as the spiritual kingdom of the Messiah, great David's greater Son (Amos 9:11,12). In the next chapter, the prophet will describe the character and rule of this restored dominion of the house of David.

Exile and return

⁹ Why do you now cry aloud—
    have you no king?
Has your counselor perished,
    that pain seizes you like that of a woman in labor?
¹⁰ Writhe in agony, O Daughter of Zion,
    like a woman in labor,
for now you must leave the city
    to camp in the open field.
You will go to Babylon;
    there you will be rescued.
There the LORD will redeem you
    out of the hand of your enemies.

The prophet has painted a glowing picture of the future, incomparable glory of the New Testament church. Before that great day comes, however, the Lord's faithful in the Old Testament church would have to undergo the bitter humiliation of exile and captivity.

Micah pictures the Israelites crying and wailing at the horror of impending doom. When two of her kings—Jehoiachin and then Zedekiah—were dragged off to Babylon (2 Kings 24,25), the grieving people lost their protector and counselor, the one who should have prepared them for the ordeal ahead.

Israel was now like a woman in labor. She writhed in almost unbearable pain at the prospect of leaving the security of Jerusalem, only to be forced to camp out as captives in the open and unprotected fields of Babylon. But then she would experience overpowering joy like that of a mother who forgets the pangs of labor in the joy over her newborn child (John 16:21). Exiled Israel's great joy would be this: "There you will be rescued. There the LORD will redeem you out of the hand of your enemies."

Luther's comments on verse 10 are worth noting:

> A great and eternal kingdom was going to be raised up, but first its birth had to happen. This birth could not happen without the great sadness and travail which generally occurs to those giving birth. . . . It is as if he [Micah] were saying: "Hold out! Endure it—however great the pain may be. A wonderful child is about to be born. Bear the hand of the Lord. Without doubt He will rescue you, and you will produce abundant fruit."
> (*Luther's Works,* Volume 18, pages 243,244)

The Lord's instrument for returning the Jews from exile would be Cyrus, the Persian king who brought down the

Babylonian Empire about 536 B.C. Shortly thereafter, God moved him to authorize the first return of the exiles.

Micah's first and only mention of Babylon by name is here in verse 10. What is surprising about the reference is that at Micah's time Babylon was only a second-rate power, a vassal of Assyria. God permitted Micah to look a century ahead to the time when Babylon would overcome Assyria and become the powerful nation that took Judah into exile.

Victory for the Daughter of Zion

> ¹¹ **But now many nations**
> **are gathered against you.**
> **They say, "Let her be defiled,**
> **let our eyes gloat over Zion!"**
> ¹² **But they do not know**
> **the thoughts of the LORD;**
> **they do not understand his plan,**
> **he who gathers them like sheaves to the threshing floor.**
> ¹³ **"Rise and thresh, O Daughter of Zion,**
> **for I will give you horns of iron;**
> **I will give you hoofs of bronze**
> **and you will break to pieces many nations."**
> **You will devote their ill-gotten gains to the LORD,**
> **their wealth to the Lord of all the earth.**

Here the prophet sees his people shortly before their capture. Gathered against them are the "many nations" that made up Nebuchadnezzar's Babylonian army as well as Israel's hostile neighbors, such as the Edomites, Moabites, and Ammonites (2 Kings 24:1,2). With eyes gloating over the prospect of victory, they surrounded Jerusalem, as eager as jackals to pounce on their prey. "But they do not know the thoughts of the LORD." He never planned for these nations to destroy Israel. They would punish her with the destruction of her city and the exile of her people, but the people would once again return.

A century after Micah, the Lord through the prophet Jeremiah informed his people in exile of his plans for them, to give them comfort and hope until the time he delivered them (Jeremiah 29:10-14). Through Micah he assured them that after the exile he would gather all their enemies "like sheaves to the threshing floor." The Daughter of Zion, that is, the people of restored Mount Zion, will be called upon to "rise and thresh." The Messiah will give her the strength, "horns of iron," and the weapons, "hoofs of bronze," to thoroughly thresh the "many nations." This is spiritual threshing, the evangelism and mission work of the New Testament church. Through Micah, the Lord says, "Rise and thresh." Through Matthew, he says, "Go and make disciples of all nations" (Matthew 28:19). As the church proclaims God's holy law and his saving gospel, unbelievers and scoffers are swept away like chaff, while believers are gathered like wheat into God's granary of salvation. "Their ill-gotten gains" might well refer to the impressive things the nations of the world produce—money, knowledge, technology, communication and transportation systems. The church rightly "devotes" these things to the Lord by using them to spread the gospel.

The promised ruler from Bethlehem

5 Marshal your troops, O city of troops,
    for a siege is laid against us.
They will strike Israel's ruler
    on the cheek with a rod.
²"But you, Bethlehem Ephrathah,
    though you are small among the clans of Judah,
out of you will come for me
    one who will be ruler over Israel,

**whose origins are from of old,
from ancient times."**

Micah gives the setting for this remarkable messianic chapter in the opening verse. He calls upon his people to prepare for an attack and a siege, the impending siege of Jerusalem by Sennacherib in 701 B.C. The enemy would "strike Israel's ruler on the cheek," that is, humiliate him in his office. King Hezekiah was forced to pay tribute to the Assyrians. Other kings of Judah were humiliated by the enemy. Manasseh, Jehoiachin, and Zedekiah were all hauled off to Babylon in shackles. The shameful and painful exile followed, a thousand miles away from home. Conditions did not improve much after the return from Babylon. The people of Judah had to submit to the power of Persia, then to Alexander and the Greeks, finally to Rome. The scepter of ruling power had departed from Judah. All that was left of a once great nation was a stump of Jesse, the royal family of King David (Isaiah 11:1).

At such a time of deep humiliation and degradation, the Messiah would come! His birthplace would be Bethlehem of the clan of Ephrathah, to distinguish it from the other Bethlehem in Zebulun, up near Nazareth (Joshua 19:15). Bethlehem had a notable history. Benjamin, a son of Jacob, was born near the town; his mother, Rachel, was buried here. Ruth gleaned the fields of Boaz at Bethlehem; here King David was born. Yet Bethlehem had remained a small town, too small to be named among the more than one hundred cities belonging to the clans of Judah (Joshua 15:20-62).

The Hebrew word translated as "clan" is also the word for the number 1,000. Hence the familiar King James translation, "little among the thousands of Judah." This, however, is not a good translation. The number 1,000 was also used for a

Bethlehem

tabulation figure in censuses and enumerations. Accordingly, 1,000 could represent either a military unit of 1,000 soldiers or a clan of 1,000 families. When Matthew quotes Micah in 2:6 of his book, he translates "rulers" in place of "clans." He may have read a Hebrew word meaning "chiefs, rulers," quite similar in spelling to "clans." The NIV footnote suggests the same possibility. The translation "clans," however, is the correct one in Micah. Bethlehem was too small to be listed as a clan-city of Judah.

In God's eyes, however, Bethlehem was anything but small. In this little village One would be born who would "come for me," that is, come to carry out the Father's saving will. He would rule "over" Israel as her spiritual king, not just "in" Israel as her earthly ruler. His purpose was to establish in place of the fallen former kingdom of David (4:8) the new kingdom of David's descendant, the Messiah. Therefore, he would be born in Bethlehem, the city of David. Unlike David, however, this promised king would have no beginning, because his "origins are from of old," in the timelessness of eternity. He is the eternal Son of God (John 8:58).

> **³ Therefore Israel will be abandoned**
>   **until the time when she who is in labor gives birth**
> **and the rest of his brothers return**
>   **to join the Israelites.**
> **⁴ He will stand and shepherd his flock**
>   **in the strength of the LORD,**
>   **in the majesty of the name of the LORD his God.**
> **And they will live securely, for then his greatness**
>   **will reach to the ends of the earth.**
> **⁵**   **And he will be their peace.**

Micah summarizes what he had been saying: "Israel will be abandoned" to foreign rule (see verse 1). Not until then will the Savior be born. Some Bible scholars refer "she who is in labor" to the Israelites in exile (4:9,10). A better reference is to Christ's virgin birth (Isaiah 7:14). The "return" of "the rest of his brothers" refers again to the return of the spiritual remnant to join the New Testament church. (See 2:12; 4:6,7,10; 5:7,8.)

As Micah mentioned already in 2:12, the Messiah will rule over the church as a shepherd tends his flock. His "strength" will be that of the Lord because he is almighty God (Isaiah 9:6). His "majesty" will be found in the name of the Lord because he is the eternal Son of God. As the Good Shepherd, he knows his sheep by name, gives his life for them, and tenderly cares for them all, young and old (John 10). Therefore, "they will live securely" with him since there is none greater than he in all the earth. With his almighty power the Messiah will defend his church and provide for it in every way.

"And he will be their peace." Only three short words in the Hebrew, but what a grand and glorious message they proclaim! Millions of words cannot exhaust their full meaning. Nor can the lifetime of a child of God experience their full joy. He will be our Peace, our Shalom, the One through whom we have a relationship of complete unity, perfect harmony, and peace with our heavenly Father. The Savior's atoning death made peace between God and us guilty sinners (Ephesians 2:14). His daily intercession with the Father gives us peace of conscience (Romans 8:33,34). His shepherd's love and guardian care allow us to live in peace in this vale of tears (Psalm 23; Romans 8:35-39). His death and resurrection will provide peace in the hour of our death (John 11:25,26). No wonder the angels outside Bethlehem announced his birth with their heavenly chorus: "Glory to God in the highest, and on earth peace to men on whom his favor rests" (Luke 2:14).

Deliverance and destruction

> When the Assyrian invades our land
>   and marches through our fortresses,
> we will raise against him seven shepherds,
>   even eight leaders of men.
> 6 They will rule the land of Assyria with the sword,
>   the land of Nimrod with drawn sword.
> He will deliver us from the Assyrian
>   when he invades our land
>   and marches into our borders.

Micah had indirectly referred to Assyria earlier in his prophecy (1:16; 2:10) as the world power threatening Judah. Now for the first time he mentions the name of this world power. Here, however, he uses the name symbolically, along with Nimrod, the founder of Babylon (Genesis 10:8-12), to refer to all powers in this world that threaten God's people. This would include not only political enemies but also forces such as the papacy, communism, rationalism, modernism, humanism, and atheism. The church's defense will be to raise up "seven shepherds, even eight leaders" against the enemy. The numbers are not to be taken mathematically but rhetorically, to express an endless number. Seven is the number of completeness; eight means there will be more than enough. Therefore, by seven and eight Micah says "enough and more," that is, without number. (For similar number uses, see Ecclesiastes 11:2; Amos 1:3; Isaiah 17:6; and Job 5:19.)

These shepherds are the spiritual leaders of the church. With "the sword of the Spirit, which is the word of God" (Ephesians 6:17), they will deliver the church from its spiritual enemies by fighting for the truth of God's Word. One thinks of Paul and the other apostles defending the fledgling New Testament church in a world of hostile false religions.

Or of Wycliffe, Luther, Tyndale, and others who sought to reform the church when it was burdened by the traditions and false teachings of men. Or of missionaries who defend the faith on foreign soil, of pastors, teachers, and professors in our Christian schools who promote and defend the faith at home. Or of Christian fathers and mothers who support and defend the truth by teaching it to their children who must grow up in a society becoming more godless every day. May God continue to raise up an endless army of faithful Christians willing "to contend for the faith that was once for all entrusted to the saints" (Jude 3)! For it is through them, and us, that Jesus Christ, the Good Shepherd and the head of the church, "will deliver us from the Assyrian."

> ⁷ **The remnant of Jacob will be**
> **in the midst of many peoples**
> **like dew from the LORD,**
> **like showers on the grass,**
> **which do not wait for man**
> **or linger for mankind.**
> ⁸ **The remnant of Jacob will be among the nations,**
> **in the midst of many peoples,**
> **like a lion among the beasts of the forest,**
> **like a young lion among flocks of sheep,**
> **which mauls and mangles as it goes,**
> **and no one can rescue.**
> ⁹ **Your hand will be lifted up in triumph over your enemies,**
> **and all your foes will be destroyed.**

Wherever the prophet has made mention of "the remnant," he has followed by showing the blessings they have as members of Christ's church (2:12; 4:6,7,10; 5:3). He does the same here. First, God's people are like the invigorating dew and rain the Lord sends upon the earth. Through the gospel they proclaim by word and deed, Christians everywhere shower the refreshing grace of God upon the barren hearts

of people, that they might become fruitful branches growing out of Christ the vine. But dew and rain "do not wait
for man." Man must make use of them when they are present, or like a passing shower they will be gone.

Therefore, the Lord has a second function for his remnant "among the nations." It is to be a lion that "mauls and
mangles as it goes." Micah had previously mentioned how
the church defends itself against all enemies by the sword
of the Word (verses 5,6). Now he refers to the negative
effect of the church's proclamation of the Word. Where the
dew and rain of the gospel have been ignored or rejected,
there the church must proclaim God's law, thundering
down like a storm with judgment and death: "Whoever
does not believe will be condemned" (Mark 16:16). That is
certain and eternal death from which "no one can rescue."

Truly, Christ's church must grieve over every soul lost
to hell and damnation. Yet the sad fact that unbelief results
in damnation is a confirmation of the church's faith in
Christ for salvation. In this sense, the church can be said to
lift up her hands in triumph over her enemies.

Cleansing Israel

¹⁰"In that day," declares the LORD,

"I will destroy your horses from among you
  and demolish your chariots.
¹¹ I will destroy the cities of your land
  and tear down all your strongholds.
¹² I will destroy your witchcraft
  and you will no longer cast spells.
¹³ I will destroy your carved images
  and your sacred stones from among you;
you will no longer bow down
  to the work of your hands.
¹⁴ I will uproot from among you your Asherah poles
  and demolish your cities.

**¹⁵ I will take vengeance in anger and wrath
upon the nations that have not obeyed me."**

The Lord has great plans for his people, the remnant. But before it can be blessed by him and become a blessing to the nations, it must first be taught "to act justly and to love mercy and to walk humbly with your God" (6:8).

In this section Micah declares the Lord's will to purge Israel of everything by which she had sought to assert herself and find security apart from God. She had considered her horses and chariots, her fortified cities and strongholds to be her strength for aggression and her defense from oppression. They must go! Israel must learn to put her trust in the Lord who is her "refuge and strength, an ever-present help in trouble" (Psalm 46:1). Israel must also learn to find her spiritual counsel and help alone in the Lord, the God of her salvation. Accordingly, the Lord would remove her witchcraft used for fortune-telling, her sorcerers who cast spells, her carved idols, her sacred stones used for idols, and her Asherah poles. These last items were wooden poles or pillars erected as idols and dedicated to Asherah, the Canaanite goddess of fertility. The worship of Asherah, often together with her male counterpart, Baal, was associated with some of the vilest and most sordid forms of sensuality.

All must go, for the Lord's honor was at stake, the salvation of his people was at stake, and the fulfillment of his gospel promise through them was at stake. Therefore, in his righteous anger he would take vengeance upon Israel and any other nation that did not obey him.

The lessons in chapter 5 are clear and appropriate. The church's weapons are not earthly but spiritual: faith, truth, the gospel (Ephesians 6:10-18). Likewise, the source of its strength is in the Lord and his Word, not in its members or in its organizational politics. These simple truths are so easily forgotten when congregations and church bodies become too concerned with statistics, public opinion polls, and head counts. It is to be feared that some church leaders, and members as well, may be more concerned with public image and acceptance than they are with God's approval. This concern unfortunately may dictate the means and methods they employ in carrying out the Lord's work. Everyone in the church will do well to remember that the Lord's battles have never been won by numbers. Gideon learned that truth when with only 300 men, he defeated 135,000 Midianites (Judges 7). Martin Luther learned it too, at Worms. The sword of the Spirit, God's infallible Word, is the church's sole weapon of offense and defense, the only means to carry out its assignment.

PART THREE

The Lord's Case against Israel and Israel's Repentance
(6:1–7:20)

In chapters 4 and 5, Micah had spoken about the glory of Israel's future, the establishment of the New Testament church through the Messiah. In chapter 6, Micah returns to the present and immediate future. As God's spokesman, he had to rebuke God's people for their wickedness. His method was to depict a courtroom scene portraying the case the Lord had against Israel.

The Lord's case against Israel

6 Listen to what the LORD says:

"Stand up, plead your case before the mountains;
    let the hills hear what you have to say.
² Hear, O mountains, the LORD's accusation;
    listen, you everlasting foundations of the earth.
For the LORD has a case against his people;
    he is lodging a charge against Israel.

³ "My people, what have I done to you?
    How have I burdened you? Answer me.
⁴ I brought you up out of Egypt
    and redeemed you from the land of slavery.
I sent Moses to lead you,
    also Aaron and Miriam.
⁵ My people, remember
    what Balak king of Moab counseled
    and what Balaam son of Beor answered.

**Remember your journey from Shittim to Gilgal,
that you may know the righteous acts of the LORD."**

The Lord is presenting his case before the mountains and hills. They are to serve as the judge and jury because they have witnessed both the Lord's goodness to Israel and Israel's unfaithfulness to the Lord. Mount Sinai saw the Lord enter into a covenant relationship with Israel (Exodus 19:1-7). Through thousands of worship services on Mount Zion, the Savior drew near to his people and drew them near to him. And the many hills in ancient Canaan blushed with shame as they watched faithless Israel practicing idolatry on their very summits (1 Kings 14:23).

Although the Israelites had forfeited his love and mercy by repeatedly breaking his covenant, the Lord still called them "my people." He refused to turn his back on them. He simply couldn't. He loved them. They were his covenant people. From them, in the fullness of time, the promised Messiah would come. But because he cared for them, he had to bring charges against them, that they might be convicted and in penitence return to him.

The Lord's lead-off questions were pivotal to his case: "'My people, what have I done to you? How have I burdened you' that you have turned against me and broken my covenant? Can you mention even one instance where I was not faithful and just with you?"

It was a case, then, of God's faithfulness versus his people's unfaithfulness. Israel stood mute before the mountains and hills because she could not answer the Lord's charge. Accordingly, the Lord presented evidence of his faithfulness. As he had promised, he had delivered his people from bitter slavery in Egypt. In addition, through the Passover celebration that began the exodus journey, the Lord had given them a beautiful preview of their spiritual deliverance from sin by Christ, the Passover Lamb (1 Corinthians 5:7).

Furthermore, God had provided his people with three excellent leaders during their 40-year wilderness journey. Moses was God's spokesman and their leader; Aaron was the high priest and his brother's spokesman to the people; their sister Miriam was a prophetess for them (Exodus 15:20).

Yet there was more! As the Israelites drew near to their promised homeland, King Balak of Moab tried to harm Israel by hiring the heathen prophet Balaam to curse them. The Lord, however, commanded Balaam to bless the Israelites—four times in fact, and one time he even proclaimed a messianic prophecy (Numbers 22–24). According to his promise to protect his people, the Lord had delivered them from the hands of evil men like Balak and Balaam.

And could Israel forget Shittim and Gilgal? Shittim lay east of Jericho, across the Jordan River. It was Israel's last camping place before crossing the Jordan and entering Canaan. Here the people had committed sexual sins with the Moabites and had joined in their idolatry. Although the Lord punished them for these sins, he had not rejected them. When the Israelites had crossed the Jordan River and set up camp at Gilgal, between the Jordan and Jericho, they knew that at last they were home. The Lord had brought his people home, into the Promised Land, just as he had promised.

The Lord did all this that Israel might know "the righteous acts of the LORD": the righteousness of his law in punishing their sin, the righteousness of his gospel in forgiving their sin, the righteousness of his promise to bring them safely into Canaan. The Lord rested his case.

Israel's reply

> ⁶ **With what shall I come before the LORD**
> **and bow down before the exalted God?**

> **Shall I come before him with burnt offerings,**
> **with calves a year old?**
> [7] **Will the LORD be pleased with thousands of rams,**
> **with ten thousand rivers of oil?**
> **Shall I offer my firstborn for my transgression,**
> **the fruit of my body for the sin of my soul?**

As the defendants in God's courtroom, the Israelites did not present much of a defense. Really, they could make no defense. They stood convicted. They had been unfaithful time and again. But did they come before the Lord on bended knee asking for mercy and forgiveness? Did they make even the faintest plea? On the contrary, in a tone of self-righteous pride, the Israelites asked God *what they had to do* to get back into his good graces. They still thought they could earn God's good will. They were willing to bargain with God as though he were one of their own corrupt judges who could be bribed to overlook their failings (3:9,11).

And what did they offer the Lord? The best of their possessions, year-old calves used in the burnt offering. Or, if quantity was what God wanted, how about thousands of rams and ten thousand rivers of oil, poured out on God's altar as an offering? If that was not sufficient, would God perhaps accept the sacrifice of their firstborn, the most precious of their possessions?

The sacrifice of children was practiced by ancient heathen peoples, especially by the Moabites and the Phoenicians (2 Kings 3:26,27). Those Israelites like wicked Ahaz (2 Kings 16:3) and godless Manasseh (2 Kings 21:6) who resorted to human sacrifice were following the practice of the heathen. There is no record of the Israelites engaging in this practice as a regular course (note, however, Ezekiel 20:25,26). In God's eyes, human sacrifice was an abominable sin forbidden under penalty of death (Leviticus 20:2-5).

The guilty Israelites of Micah's day were willing to do anything to please God—except what he wanted. He desired "mercy, not sacrifice" (Matthew 9:13). He wanted the sacrifice of "a broken and contrite heart" (Psalm 51:17). Therefore, Micah answered Israel,

> **⁸ He has showed you, O man, what is good.**
> **And what does the LORD require of you?**
> **To act justly and to love mercy**
> **and to walk humbly with your God.**

The Israelites should have known what is good, what the Lord required of them for a right relationship with him. He had shown them through his prophets. First, "act justly," that is, act according to God's standard of justice as laid out in his law. Worshiping God alone and not idols, trusting in him alone and not in weapons or in man is acting justly toward God. Acting justly to one's fellow-man is showing others no injustice or cruelty in word or deed but treating them like oneself. Do you recognize the Ten Commandments here?

Second, "love mercy." Again, this is God's kind of mercy. It's the love he shows to us, a forgiving, compassionate love, an unselfish, giving love. The father of the prodigal son had it; he welcomed his son back with open arms. The good Samaritan showed it to the hapless victim along the road. Do you recognize the Ten Commandments again?

Third, "walk humbly with your God." God-pleasing humility is found only in the presence of the holy and just God. When people see themselves as God sees them, as sinners deserving death, as imperfect creatures of dust and clay, then they will humbly seek God's forgiveness in Christ and gladly seek his help to live godly lives according to his will. Again, do you recognize the Ten Commandments?

157

Micah 6:8 is really an epitome of the entire Law, of both tables, which show our duty to God and our duty to our neighbor (Matthew 22:37-40).

Some people like to quote Micah 6:8 to state what they feel are the essentials of religion. But unless these people realize that these requirements of God's law are impossible for the unregenerate to fulfill, they are actually promoting a religion of work-righteousness. Penitent faith in the Savior is the basis for showing justice, mercy, and humility as God requires. Faith gives us the reason and the gospel gives us the strength to love the Lord our God above all else and our neighbor as ourselves.

An interesting sidenote: Micah 6:8 appears as a motto in the alcove of religion in the reading room of the Library of Congress in Washington, D.C.

Israel's guilt and punishment

⁹ Listen! The LORD is calling to the city—
   and to fear your name is wisdom—
   "Heed the rod and the One who appointed it.
¹⁰ Am I still to forget, O wicked house,
   your ill-gotten treasures
   and the short ephah, which is accursed?
¹¹ Shall I acquit a man with dishonest scales,
   with a bag of false weights?
¹² Her rich men are violent;
   her people are liars
   and their tongues speak deceitfully.

The Lord has presented his case against Israel. She had no defense and was guilty. Now she had to stand before the Lord and hear her just sentence.

The Lord addressed the city of Jerusalem, representing all of the nation of Judah, as the center of her sinful practices (1:5). The prophet reminded the people that it is godly wisdom to fear the Lord's name, to know that his ways are always just, even his judgments, and that he would rather forgive than punish. The rod of his punishment is Assyria, now threatening to invade Israel. The Lord has "appointed it" this way. All nations are instruments in his hand, unwittingly carrying out both his judgments and his plan of salvation.

Israel's sins and wickedness that call for punishment have been referred to earlier in chapters 2 and 3. Now Micah points out more of these sins, particularly those that produce illicit wealth. Greedy merchants gave short measure and used dishonest scales—practices the Lord soundly denounced (Deuteronomy 25:13-16; Amos 8:5). "Her rich men"—the greedy landowners, corrupt judges, and heartless rulers—resorted to lies and false accusations, dishonest contracts, and strong-arm violence to acquire property and funds. What a sharp contrast to the things God requires: justice, mercy, and humility (verse 8)!

> ¹³ **Therefore, I have begun to destroy you,**
> **to ruin you because of your sins.**
> ¹⁴ **You will eat but not be satisfied;**
> **your stomach will still be empty.**
> **You will store up but save nothing,**
> **because what you save I will give to the sword.**
> ¹⁵ **You will plant but not harvest;**
> **you will press olives but not use the oil on yourselves,**
> **you will crush grapes but not drink the wine.**
> ¹⁶ **You have observed the statutes of Omri**
> **and all the practices of Ahab's house,**
> **and you have followed their traditions.**
> **Therefore I will give you over to ruin**
> **and your people to derision;**
> **you will bear the scorn of the nations."**

In the mind of God, Israel's judgment had already begun. He knew what would happen. Fields would become barren as a curse for the people's sins (Deuteronomy 28:15-18). What food they might find would provide little nourishment. When Assyria and Babylon invaded the land, they would follow the practice of conquerors and devastate the land while destroying its produce (Joel 1:5-12). Empty stomachs, barren fields, food wantonly destroyed—a horrible famine would stalk the land (Jeremiah 52:6).

But the famine of their faith was worse. It was clear that they had not been following the commands of the Lord. Whose commands, then, had they been keeping? Those of Omri and Ahab, described in 1 Kings chapter 16 as worse than any previous kings in Israel, the Northern Kingdom. Omri was the founder of Samaria and of the idolatrous house of Ahab, his son. It was Ahab who introduced the worship of Baal and Asherah as the national religion of Israel (16:31-33). He also persecuted the prophets (18:4) and was guilty of robbery and murder (chapter 21).

Exactly what the sinful "statutes of Omri" were, we are not told, but Judah followed them as well as the evil practices of Ahab. For this reason the Lord would judge his people by turning them over to the invader to be ruined and to become objects of scorn. The nations among whom they would live in exile would deride them for being God's people dispersed among foreigners (Ezekiel 36:20). There is no bright side to the picture of sin. God can only see sin for what it is and punish it.

In the final chapter of his book, Micah brings his prophecy to a grand climax. The Lord's case against Israel must stand. The chosen nation deserved God's punishment and would receive it. But not every Israelite had bowed his knee to idols or given his heart over to the love of money. Just as there would be a believing remnant in the Babylonian exile, so there was in Israel a penitent remnant of the Lord's people. It is as their spokesman that Micah speaks the words of chapter 7.

Israel's lament and repentance

7 What misery is mine!
    I am like one who gathers summer fruit
        at the gleaning of the vineyard;
    there is no cluster of grapes to eat,
        none of the early figs that I crave.
² The godly have been swept from the land;
        not one upright man remains.
    All men lie in wait to shed blood;
        each hunts his brother with a net.
³ Both hands are skilled in doing evil;
        the ruler demands gifts,
    the judge accepts bribes,
        the powerful dictate what they desire—
    they all conspire together.

Micah was miserable as he looked at Israel. He looked for fruits of repentance but didn't see any. God's people resembled a vineyard that was no longer producing fruit (Isaiah 5:1-7). "The godly" and the "upright man" were no more to be seen. They had either gone into hiding because their lives were not safe among the ungodly in Israel, or they had joined their ranks. Instead of justice, mercy, and humility, the prophet saw lovelessness and bloodshed everywhere. Like hunters lying in wait with their nets, the majority in Israel tried to obtain the property of others by threats and entrapments.

And they were good at it, developing all their abilities—using both hands, as it were—to a high degree. The rulers always needed more money and had learned to get it by exorbitant taxes. Greedy judges became rich by accepting bribes. People of influence and power got what they wanted simply by demanding it, or else! Realizing the strength that lay in their numbers, all of them became accomplices in their wickedness.

⁴ **The best of them is like a brier,**
the most upright worse than a thorn hedge.
The day of your watchmen has come,
the day God visits you.
Now is the time of their confusion.
⁵ **Do not trust a neighbor;**
put no confidence in a friend.
Even with her who lies in your embrace
be careful of your words.
⁶ **For a son dishonors his father,**
a daughter rises up against her mother,
a daughter-in-law against her mother-in-law—
a man's enemies are the members of his own household.

Micah compares his greedy and lawless countrymen to thorns in a lowly brier patch. Even the best of them had no moral uprightness anymore. They were fit only to be burned like thorns (See 2 Samuel 23:6,7).

Therefore, "the day of your watchmen has come," the day predicted by Israel's prophetic watchmen when God's judgment would strike (Jeremiah 6:17-19). Because his people had rejected the warnings of his prophets, they would have only confusion when God's judgment came crashing down on them. They would not know what to expect. As a matter of fact, Israel was already tasting his judgment by living in a godless and wicked society of their own making.

Micah drew them a picture of the tragic results of their sin. Normal human relationships of trust and love were nonexistent. One didn't dare trust neighbor or friend anymore, not even one's wife or husband. Even parents and children viewed one another with suspicion, ready to deceive the other for personal gain. The home had lost its foundation of love, honor, and respect.

Things in the nation of Israel had come to such a wretched state of affairs that "a man's enemies are the members of his own household." The root cause was to be found in the heart, the cesspool where all sin originates (Matthew 15:19). Greed and covetousness, not being satisfied or content and wanting more than what God has provided—doesn't this cover most sins, from idolatry (wanting more security) to adultery (wanting more sex)? Money can be a blessing from God, but "the love of money is a root of all kinds of evil" (1 Timothy 6:10). The wickedness of Israel's society and the breakdown of the homes of Israel centered in the sinful desire for more money and for more power and prestige. Once these become acceptable goals for people, any method becomes a justifiable means to the end.

Micah 7:2-6 reads almost like today's newspaper. These verses are an indictment of our own times. If only people today would learn that wealth is not everything, that there is greater joy to be had in being "rich toward God" (Luke 12:21). When any society reaches this stage of corruption, the judgment of God is near at hand.

In verses 1 to 6, Micah has not merely been lamenting the sorry consequences of Israel's sin. Speaking for the remnant of believers in her midst, he also has been acknowledging any sins on their part. Israel's penitence and faith become evident in the next section.

Israel's confident hope in the Lord

> [7] But as for me, I watch in hope for the LORD,
>   I wait for God my Savior;
>   my God will hear me.
>
> [8] Do not gloat over me, my enemy!
>   Though I have fallen, I will rise.
>   Though I sit in darkness,
>   the LORD will be my light.

⁹ **Because I have sinned against him,**
 I will bear the LORD's wrath,
until he pleads my case
 and establishes my right.
He will bring me out into the light;
 I will see his righteousness.
¹⁰ **Then my enemy will see it**
 and will be covered with shame,
she who said to me,
 "Where is the LORD your God?"
My eyes will see her downfall;
 even now she will be trampled underfoot
 like mire in the streets.

This is a key passage in the final chapter—indeed, in the entire prophecy of Micah! Identifying himself completely with the nation of Israel, Micah confessed his sin and admitted the rightness of God's judgment. He also expressed his trust in the Lord's deliverance.

Penitent Israel could be certain that the Lord had brought about her affliction. She could be just as certain that God would deliver her. "I watch in hope" has the meaning to keep on watching intently. This is faith-watching, a looking and hoping even though reason says, "No way!" (see Hebrews 11:1). Israel was to keep watching for the Lord, waiting for "God my Savior" to bring deliverance from her sin and from exile. The believing Israelite had every reason to maintain this hope. God had given his promise (4:10). He would hear and answer Israel's plea for forgiveness and deliverance.

Even though Assyria and Babylon would gloat over her fallen condition, believing Israel was confident that the Lord would raise her up again. She confessed her sin without making excuses. She acknowledged that she had deserved God's wrath. Instead of complaining, she humbly submitted to the

Lord's will and accepted her affliction in exile not as punishment, but as discipline from the Lord who loved her (Hebrews 12:6). In the dark night of his grief, Job expressed the same confident faith: "Though he slay me, yet will I hope in him" (Job 13:15).

It was such confident faith and hope in her Savior that would sustain Israel during the 70 years of exile in Babylon. In the darkness of her affliction, she would see the light of her salvation in the Messiah. Even if exile meant walking through the valley of the shadow of death, Israel would have no fear. She knew the Lord would bring her "out into the light" of a new and better life. Throughout it all, penitent Israel would "see his righteousness," knowing that the Lord was just in chastening her with exile for her sins and merciful in laying her sins upon the Messiah to bear their punishment. And there was still more. Israel would know the Messiah as her advocate to plead her case before the Father, ensuring her forgiveness and her right to be called his people.

Israel's enemies would taunt her in her exile by saying, "Where is the Lord your God?"—a common jeer of the ungodly when they see Christians afflicted (Psalm 42:3; Joel 2:17). But their mockery would become their shame, like the mud and mire in the streets, when they would see how God delivered his people.

God would not let his people down. He had great plans for them.

> **¹¹ The day for building your walls will come,**
> **the day for extending your boundaries.**
> **¹² In that day people will come to you**
> **from Assyria and the cities of Egypt,**
> **even from Egypt to the Euphrates**
> **and from sea to sea**
> **and from mountain to mountain.**

¹³ The earth will become desolate because of its inhabitants, as the result of their deeds.

The reference here is not to rebuilding the walls of Jerusalem after the Jews returned from exile. Rather, the Lord is promising to build the walls of his New Testament church by extending its boundaries (Zechariah 10:9,10). During the centuries before Christ came, God's church consisted mostly of members of the Jewish nation. "In that day," in the messianic era (4:1,6; 5:10), it would become a universal church without boundaries, "from sea to sea and from mountain to mountain," a church for all people, even for past enemies who would repent. As believers of all races and nations come to the church, "the earth will become desolate," with only unbelievers left, whom the Lord has deserted for rejecting his gospel (5:15).

The Lord had promised to enlarge his church (4:1-5; Isaiah 11:10-16). Today we can see how he is keeping his promise. The church founded on Jesus Christ spans the globe. Through its preaching of the gospel it seeks to reach out to as many as possible before the end time comes when all mission work must cease (Matthew 24:14). Lord, give us strength and zeal to work while it is still day, before the night comes when no man can work!

Israel's prayer and praise

Grateful for her forgiveness and restoration, penitent Israel now breaks forth in a prayer of joyful praise.

¹⁴ Shepherd your people with your staff,
 the flock of your inheritance,
which lives by itself in a forest,
 in fertile pasturelands.
Let them feed in Bashan and Gilead
 as in days long ago.

Micah had already used the figure of a shepherd to describe the Messiah's role (2:12; 4:8). Now Micah prayed for him to lead his flock with the staff of his Word. The staff was used to lead the sheep to refreshing waters and green pastures (Psalm 23), to prod the lagging, to bring back the straying, to ward off the wolves, and to return the sheep to shelter. So Christ is asked to lead and defend his church, "which lives by itself in a forest" of unbelievers. The little flock needs his help and the "fertile pasturelands" of his Word! Bashan and Gilead, east of the Sea of Galilee and along the Jordan River, were both fine grazing lands. For that reason the tribes of Reuben, Gad, and half of Manasseh had requested permission to settle there "in days long ago," when Israel entered Canaan (Numbers 32). Here they stand for the rich and wholesome food the soul finds in God's Word.

The Lord's answer

> ¹⁵ **"As in the days when you came out of Egypt,**
> **I will show them my wonders."**

When the Lord rescued his people from bondage in Egypt, he performed so many great miracles that it became a unique period in Israel's history (Deuteronomy 34:10-12; Joshua 24:2-18). God used the exodus and his miracles to establish Israel as his Old Testament covenant people. But now, when he delivers his remnant out of exile, he will establish his New Testament church with far greater miracles, all of them centering in Christ: his virgin birth, his death as the Son of God, his resurrection and ascension. The New Testament people of God are therefore rightly called the Christian church.

The prayer of Israel continues with praise for the Lord's blessing on his church.

> ¹⁶ **Nations will see and be ashamed,**
>   **deprived of all their power.**
> **They will lay their hands on their mouths**
>   **and their ears will become deaf.**
> ¹⁷ **They will lick dust like a snake,**
>   **like creatures that crawl on the ground.**
> **They will come trembling out of their dens;**
>   **they will turn in fear to the LORD our God**
>   **and will be afraid of you.**

When nations see the Lord's mighty New Testament miracles and his great salvation in Christ, they will "be ashamed." Like all unbelievers, they have always placed confidence in their own power and wealth, their statesmanship and military strength, their technology and wisdom. What has it gained them? Nothing but trouble, fightings, and wars within and without. They will be ashamed when they realize how powerless they really are and how powerful the Lord and his gospel are.

With "hands on their mouths" to show their reverential silence and astonishment (Job 21:5), with their ears deaf to any further boasting, they will come in subjection to the Lord like snakes licking the dust. Leaving "their dens" of good works and merit by which they had hoped to escape God's judgment, the people moved by the gospel will come to the Lord in penitential fear, seeking his forgiveness. They will have learned the blessed truth about Christ and his church that all redeemed have learned: "Salvation is found in no one else, for there is no other name under heaven given to men by which we must be saved" (Acts 4:12).

The church's hymn of praise

¹⁸ Who is a God like you,
who pardons sin and forgives the transgression
of the remnant of his inheritance?
You do not stay angry forever
but delight to show mercy.
¹⁹ You will again have compassion on us;
you will tread our sins underfoot
and hurl all our iniquities into the depths of the sea.
²⁰ You will be true to Jacob,
and show mercy to Abraham,
as you pledged on oath to our fathers
in days long ago.

The Lord has assured penitent Israel of his forgiveness and of his deliverance of the remnant from exile. He has promised Israel that her remnant will become his church of the New Testament, drawing members from far and wide, where all will find forgiveness, life, and salvation in the Savior.

After all that, Israel cannot contain herself. "Who is a God like you?" Is this perhaps a play on the prophet's name, Micah, which means "Who is like the Lord?" At any rate, Micah raises the rhetorical question to show that there is absolutely none like God, because he forgives sins (mentioned four times), he is compassionate (four times), and he is faithful (two times).

Our sins are our offenses against God's holy will; our transgressions are our stubborn rebellion and perverseness before God. It makes no difference what they are or how many there are—God forgives them all. He removes them from us and places them on his Son, who carried them to the cross. The result in picture-language is that God "tread[s] our sins underfoot" so they are dead and can no longer rise to haunt us. He hurls them "into the depths of the sea" where they can never be found again or remembered.

Complete forgiveness in Christ is God's gift to us because of his undeserved love and pity for us wretched sinners. Though angry because of our sins, he does "not stay angry forever" because Jesus permitted God's wrath over our sins to strike him instead of us.

The Lord promised his Old Testament patriarchs, Abraham, Isaac, and Jacob, that through one of their descendants he would bless all nations of the earth (Genesis 12:2,3; 15:5). In mercy he has kept that promise by offering salvation to all nations through his Son, Jesus Christ. He continues to keep that promise by daily adding to his New Testament church those who are being saved (Acts 2:47). On this high note of gospel joy, Micah brings his remarkable prophecy to a close.

We close our study of the book of Micah with this fitting quotation from *The Minor Prophets* by Charles L. Feinberg, pages 186 and 187:

> The last three verses of this book are joined to the book of Jonah for reading in the synagogue on the afternoon of the Day of Atonement. Once a year on the afternoon of New Year, the orthodox Jew goes to a running stream or river and symbolically empties his pockets of his sins into the water, while he recites verses 18-20. The service is called "Tashlich" after the Hebrew word meaning "thou wilt cast."

> By God's grace to us, you and I know this is not God's way of casting our sins into the depths of the sea. He does this for us only because of the work of the Lord Jesus Christ on Calvary where he bore those sins for us. Because he was punished for them, God can pass over the transgression of any sinner.